THE
ROLLING STONES

THIS IS A CARLTON BOOK

Published in Great Britain in 2014 by
Carlton Books Limited
20 Mortimer Street
London W1T 3JW

Previously published as *Treasures of The Rolling Stones* in 2011.

Copyright 2014 © Carlton Books Limited

A CIP catalogue for this book is available from
the British Library.

ISBN 978-1-78097-602-0

Printed in China

10 9 8 7 6 5 4 3 2 1

THE
ROLLING STONES

GLENN CROUCH

CARLTON
BOOKS

CONTENTS

INTRODUCTION

Who would have any inkling back in 1962 when the fledgling Rolling Stones started out that they would still be with us over 50 years later? For a pop act to have that kind of longevity was totally unheard of. Indeed, the band themselves didn't expect to be around for more than two or three years.

This book is a concise history of "the greatest rock 'n' roll" band in the world, from their roots in the London Blues and R'n'B scene, through the mania and scandal of the Sixties, the mega stardom of the Seventies and the mega tours through the Eighties right through to the present day.

In this book we have featured some amazing facsimiles of memorabilia and ephemera including extremely rare hand bills, tickets, set lists, promotional posters and more. I do hope you enjoy this look back through rock 'n' roll history …

Glenn Crouch, London 2014

THE EARLY YEARS

Late Fifties Britain; the draining effects of World War 2 were still apparent both in Britain's economy and certainly in the psychology of the generation that had fought in and lived through the conflict. The children who had been born during the war years were now entering their teens and eager to shake off the stifling constraints of their parents' expectations and attitudes. Many looked to America for their inspiration. US forces were still based in the UK and Western Europe and American Forces Network radio was easy to access. Jazz, and later blues, R'n'B and rock'n'roll were blasting into the homes of teenagers eager to consume the exciting and rebellious new music.

Above: Crawdaddy Club, Richmond, April 1963. **Below:** Alexis Korner, the Godfather of the British Blues movement.

Among these were a certain Michael Philip Jagger and Keith Richards, both residents of Dartford in the north-west corner of the garden of England, Kent, a mere 16 miles or so from the centre of London.

Legend has it that although the pair knew of each other, and had even attended the same primary school, they didn't really get together until they met on a train in November 1961 and Keith, spotting that Mick had some Chuck Berry records under his arm, struck up a conversation with his soon-to-be partner-in-crime. By coincidence, the pair had a mutual friend in fellow blues aficionado Dick Taylor, with whom Keith attended Sidcup Art College and with whom Mick had already formed a band, albeit one that hadn't graduated from Dick's bedroom yet.

Although he was a somewhat shy teenager, Keith's natural curiosity soon got the better of him and he plucked up courage to join in Taylor and Jagger's bedroom jam sessions, which included Mick on vocals and harmonica, Taylor on rudimentary drums and Allen Etherington on guitar.

In March 1962, having read in the *Melody Maker* that a club specializing in blues and R'n'B had opened in Ealing, West London, the band – having named themselves Little Boy Blue and the Blue Boys – made a pilgrimage from East to West and laid eyes on what was to them the astonishing sight of Alexis Korner's pick-up ensemble, Blues Incorporated. Here they met one Elmo Lewis, the *nom de guerre* of a certain Brian Jones.

Above: The group when they were still officially a sextet, with Ian Stewart holding the maracas.

Brian had been playing a wicked slide guitar with Blues Incorporated and before long he, Mick, Keith and Dick had become firm friends.

By May of that year the Blue Boys had ingratiated themselves with Korner to the extent that soon they were being invited to perform the occasional number with the band. They were in good company, for those also being welcomed on stage alongside Blues Incorporated included the likes of Paul Jones (later to front Manfred Mann) and Long John Baldry.

Brian, impressed with Mick's stage presence and vocal abilities, asked him to join the band he was putting together with Ian Stewart, Brian Knight and Geoff Bradford. Mick agreed, but with the proviso that Keith came with him. Brian agreed, but Knight and Bradford vehemently didn't, at which point Taylor was asked to join to play bass, even though up to that point he hadn't even picked up the instrument.

By mid-1962 Little Boy Blue and the Blue Boys had ditched their somewhat cumbersome moniker to become The Rollin' Stones, after one of Muddy Waters' best-known songs. The band was embarking on

a career of sorts, but paid gigs were hard to find, as was a permanent drummer. Several were tried out including Trevor Chapman, Mick Avory (later of The Kinks), and Blues Incorporated's Charlie Watts.

Chapman was in place when the band recorded a demo at Curly Clayton Sound Studios in Highbury, North London, on October 27, 1962. Legend has it that an executive at Decca Records, who heard the demo, declared that while the band showed promise, 'they'd never make it with that singer'.

By and by Dick Taylor, frustrated at having to play bass instead of guitar, decided to fly the nest. His replacement would be Bill Wyman (*né* Perks), the bassist with rock'n'roll band The Cliftons, an act with which the early Stones had often shared bills.

With the band's popularity snowballing and regular gigs now the norm (including a weekly residency at the famous Crawdaddy Club in Richmond) Trevor Chapman's unreliability was becoming a real nuisance. Eventually their relentless pursuit of Charlie Watts paid dividends and Charlie was persuaded to give up the Blues Incorporated role to throw his lot in with the Stones.

1963: THE BAND COMES ALIVE

The band soon came to the attention of Decca Records again and in particular Dick Rowe, famously the man who had turned down The Beatles. Rowe, eager not to miss out again, reluctantly agreed a recording deal with Andrew Loog Oldham, who by this time had used his not inconsiderable charm to woo the band and to persuade them that it was in their best interests that he became their manager. Oldham was an original 'mover and shaker' and had worked with Brian Epstein as a part-time publicist for The Beatles.

Such was Oldham's persuasive guile that he managed to strike a deal with Decca that gave him full control over the band's recording process, effectively licensing the finished recordings to Decca.

JUNE 7, 1963
Single: Come On c/w I Want To Be Loved (Decca F11675)

It was inevitable that the Stones would choose a Chuck Berry song to cover for their first release. Aware that they had to be commercially savvy but without selling out, a Berry number was a fairly obvious choice. However a number of his more well-known numbers had already been covered, most notably by The Beatles: so, needing a point of difference, the Stones opted for 'Come On'. The release was marked by the band appearing on TV for the first time, memorably appearing on ATV's *Thank Your Lucky Stars*, resplendent in dog-tooth jackets and collars and ties!

Below: Suited and booted – and the Vox amps are pretty smart too.

Far Left: Andrew Loog Oldham directing the band at Olympic Studios in May of 1963.

Right: A personal handwritten letter from Bill Wyman to the founder of the Stones fan club, Shirley Arnold.

ROYAL STATION HOTEL
NEWCASTLE-ON-TYNE 1

Sunday 10th Nov, 1963

Dear Shirley,

many thanks for your very nice Birthday card you sent me & letter.

Sorry if I have kept you waiting so long for a reply but there were so many to answer—that I have only just got round to it now.

I believe you got them at Hammersmith but I haven't sent you autographs as week, but if not, let me know & I shall send them next time.

Everything's going great & the new record has gone into the charts after only 1 week – hope it goes up.

Thanks again,

Bill Wyman

NOVEMBER 1, 1963

Single: I Wanna Be Your Man/Stoned (Decca F 11764)

In which The Beatles lend a hand! By the tail-end of 1963, Merseybeat, with The Beatles leading the charge, was sweeping all before it and the Stones, having struggled to come up with a commercially viable follow-up to their debut, were not about to turn away this gilt-edged opportunity for a hit, an as-yet-unreleased Lennon and McCartney song offered by the pair after Andrew Loog Oldham had poured his heart out to them following a boozy Variety Club 'do' at the Savoy.

The B-side was one of Jagger and Richard's earliest attempts at writing their own material (under the pseudonym of Nanker, Phelge) – a suitably bluesy, piano-tinged instrumental romp.

As 1963 gave way to 1964 the Stones, despite having only released two singles, were well on the way to becoming the UK's new pop phenomenon. From mid-July 1963 to the end of the year they had played well over one hundred shows, including a package tour with The Everly Brothers and Bo Diddley. They had also made six TV appearances, three on ATV's *Thank Your Lucky Stars* and three on what was considered the coolest pop show of the Sixties, *Ready Steady Go!*.

Right: The band on *Ready Steady Go!* August, 1963. Note Bill Wyman's home-made fretless bass.

IAN STEWART (1938–1985)

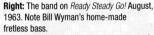

Ian Andrew Robert Stewart was born in Pittenweem, Fife, in Scotland on July 18, 1938, and raised in Sutton, Surrey.

The 'sixth Stone', Stu, as he was affectionately known, stuck with the band through thick and thin after famously being sidelined by Andrew Loog Oldham for being (in Oldham's words) 'the odd one out'.

Being somewhat older than everyone in the band apart from Bill Wyman, he was in many ways a bit of a father figure, particularly to Mick, Keith and Brian. He was certainly the organizer in the group, being the only member with access to a telephone; during working hours at his job with ICI he would take calls and handle bookings. Later on he would purchase a van, organize the gear and drive to gigs. He jokingly referred to his bandmates as 'my little three-chord wonders'.

So it came to pass that in early 1963, with the band beginning to gain momentum, Oldham made his move to oust Stu from the line-up.

Left: 'The odd one out' – Ian Stewart tinkles the ivories.

Oldham's reasoning, apart from Stu's conformist looks, was that six was too many members for a rock'n'roll band and that 'the kids' would never remember more than five members' names.

This must have been particularly crushing for Stu, but despite this he remained loyal to the cause and although not an 'official' member he was an integral part of the band's camp, right up to his sad and premature death from a heart attack in 1985.

Apart from having played piano and organ on a number of Stones releases right up to *Undercover* in 1983, Stu also appeared on Led Zeppelin's 'Rock and Roll' (*Led Zeppelin IV*, 1971) and 'Boogie With Stu', (*Physical Graffiti*, 1975) as well as on recordings by The Yardbirds, George Thorogood and the Destroyers and the 1971 *Howlin' Wolf* album (released on Rolling Stones Records) which also featured Charlie Watts, Bill Wyman and Eric Clapton, among others.

In the late Seventies he formed Rocket 88, a pick-up band which at various times also included Charlie Watts, Bob Hall, George Green, Colin Smith and John Picard among its members. A live album, recorded in Germany in 1979, was released by Atlantic Records in 1981.

NELSONS SPORTS AND SOCIAL CLUB
presents—by Public Request

TEEN·BEAT NIGHT '63

SIX HOURS NON-STOP DANCING FEATURING

FIRST TIME IN THE NORTH-WEST—BRITAIN'S TOP RHYTHM AND BLUES GROUP

THE ROLLING STONES

Decca Recording Stars—"Come On"

THE FAMOUS LIVERPOOL SOUND—DIRECT FROM THE "CAVERN," LIVERPOOL

THE MERSEYBEATS

Fontana Recording Stars—"It's Love That Really Counts"

DECCA RECORDING STARS—"TOSSING AND TURNING," "MEMPHIS, TENNESSEE"

DAVE BERRY & the CRUISERS

TWIST AND SHOUT TO THE EXCITING RHYTHM AND BLUES SOUND OF

THE DOODLE-BUGS

FLORAL HALL BALLROOM, MORECAMBE
FRIDAY, 27TH SEPTEMBER, 1963

8 p.m. to 2 a.m.

Tickets **5/-**, at the door **6/-**

BAR EXTENSION UNTIL I A.M.   LATE TRANSPORT AVAILABLE

Tickets on sale from

Floral Hall Box Office; J. M. Harris, Westgate; John B. Barber and Son Ltd., New Street, Lancaster; S. E. Taverner, 18 Slyne Road, Torrisholme; Kenneth Gardner Ltd., all branches; Plough Hotel, Galgate; or any Member of the Committee

RECORDS OF THE ABOVE ARTISTS ARE OBTAINABLE FROM KENNETH GARDNER'S

John B. Barber and Son Ltd., Lancaster

"Rock and roll ain't nothing but jazz with a hard backbeat."

Keith Richards

THIS PORTION TO BE GIVEN UP ON FRIDAY 7th AUGUST 7.30 to 10 p.m.

RICHMOND ATHLETIC ASSOCIATION GROUNDS
KEW FOOT ROAD · RICHMOND · SURREY

THE NATIONAL JAZZ FEDERATION presents the

4th NATIONAL JAZZ FESTIVAL

7th, 8th & 9th AUGUST, 1964

FRIDAY EVENING | **10/-** | № 1019

Above: National Jazz Festival ticket, August 1964.

Left: Super rare poster for a very early Rolling Stones concert in Morecambe — their first time in Britain's North-West.

Dear Melinda,

Thanks nuts for your nice letter and the sketch. Which was very good. Keep at it.

Mick is the lead of the Group. At one time I was, but Mick took over, don't ask me why. We just thought it would be better as he is a good leader.

Yes, I do like Bob Dylan. He is different, and I like people with originality!

Mick's birthday was on the 26th July.

I've had my hair long for four years or more now. I must rush dear honestly,

Brian Jones
xx

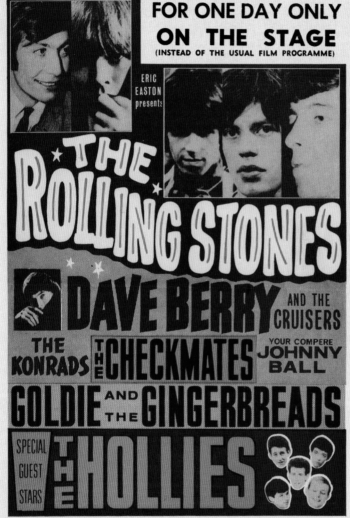

Above: Signed letter from Brian Jones to fan, 1965.

Right: ABC Romford flyer, March 1965.

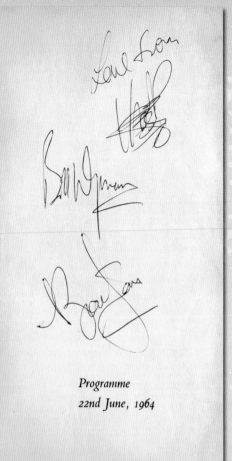

Magdalen College
Commemoration Ball

Programme
22nd June, 1964

ALBERT A. BONICI and ANDY LOTHIAN, JNR.

present

Star Parade

MARK PETERS AND THE SILHOUETTES

PETER AND GORDON

THE ROLLING STONES

FREDDIE AND THE DREAMERS

MILLIE AND THE FIVE EMBERS

DAVE BERRY AND THE CRUISERS

SOUVENIR PROGRAMME   1/6

THE ROLLING STONES

MICK JAGGER

Vocalist and harmonica player; born Dartford, Kent; age 19; Mick is in his second year at the London School of Economics, but has no idea of economics himself. He likes money and spends it like water. Also likes Chinese food, clothes, driving, the Rolling Stones, Bo Diddley, and life in general. Underneath that mousey mop sparkle two big blue eyes. Has been with the group from its birth.

BRIAN JONES

Vocalist/guitarist and harmonica player; born in Cheltenham; moved to London two years ago. Age 19. Blonde haired. Smokes 60 cigarettes a day; has experience of many jobs, including coal lorry driving; assistant in an architect's office; playing in a jazz band and a year's hitch-hiking on the Continent. Fascinated by the railways, wants to be President of the Dr Beeching Fan Club.

BILL WYMAN

Bass guitar and vocals. Hollow-cheeked Bill is 21 and is often called "The Ghost" due to his pale complexion. Interested in poetry, books, food. Another Chucky Berry fan, Bill has dark hair and hails from Beckenham, Kent.

KEITH RICHARD

Guitarist. Black-haired Keith was born in Dartford 19 years ago; worked in a post office. Has one romance in his life — his guitar! Would like a house boat on the Thames; collects Chuck Berry and Jimmy Reed records.

CHARLIE WATTS

Drums; 21 years old, Charlie is the "Beau Brummell" of the group. Has over 100 pocket handkies. "Charlie Boy," as he is called, lives in Wembley, has spent the last year between an advertising agency and the Rolling Stones.

Stone by Stone

What's in Store for the Stones?

ONE-NIGHTERS for the rest of this month, then it's off to the States for a fortnight or three weeks. That's the immediate future for the Rolling Stones. When they return from America they will begin work on their first film, and in the offing, for early next year, is a tour of Australia.

> ## "Their hair isn't long; it's just smaller foreheads and higher eyebrows."

Dean Martin's famous inspection of The Rolling Stones

1964: RIOT AND ROLL

The manic touring schedule of the latter part of 1963 and the incredible press they were now receiving had catapulted the Stones into the national consciousness: and so it was that after an appearance on New Year's Day on the first ever *Top Of The Pops*, the band embarked on their first national tour as headliners – a fourteen-date jaunt round the country with The Ronettes. This was the start of a truly hectic year in which the band would tour North America for the first time, release their debut album and score a string of massive chart successes, including their first number 1 hit in the UK.

JANUARY 17, 1964
The Rolling Stones EP (Decca DFE 8560)
Bye Bye Johnny/Money/You Better Move On/Poison Ivy

Back in the early Sixties, EPs (extended play) were an important marketing tool for the music industry, being seen as a sort of middle ground between conventional singles and LP's.

Four well-chosen cover versions adorn the band's debut EP, but it was their version of Arthur Alexander's 'You Better Move On' that really caught the record-buying public's attention and the EP was soon rocketing up the chart.

Left: Posing before a TV show in Montreaux.

Below: A very rare tour programme from the Harrow-on-the-Hill Granada, January 1964.

GRANADA

JANUARY 1964

GROUP SCENE '64
with the
RONETTES
and
ROLLING STONES

program one shilling

FEBRUARY 21, 1964
Single - Not Fade Away/Little By Little (Decca F 11845)

Hot on the heels of the success of their debut EP came the Stones' Bo Diddleyesque reworking of Buddy Holly's 'Not Fade Away'. It was a masterstroke, and launched the band into the Top 3 for the first time.

APRIL 26, 1964
The Rolling Stones (Decca LK 4605)

Route 66/I Just Want To Make Love To You/Honest I Do/I Need You Baby (Mona)/Now I've Got A Witness/Little By Little/I'm A King Bee/Carol/Tell Me (You're Coming Back)/Can I Get A Witness/You Can Make It If You Try/Walking The Dog

A rough and ready, restless, relentless rock through their early repertoire, the band's debut album is still, nearly fifty years after its release, regarded as one of their best. Raw it might be, but it perfectly encapsulated where the band were at and what they were purveying in those heady days.

Recorded over five days at Regent Sound in Denmark Street in the heart of London's West End, *The Rolling Stones* clocks in at just over thirty minutes' playing time. The Stones' influences were here for everyone to see; Jimmy Reed ('Honest I Do'), Slim Harpo ('I'm A King Bee'), Willie Dixon ('I Just Want To Make Love To You'), Chuck Berry ('Carol'), Rufus Thomas ('Walking The Dog'). There was even a nod to early Motown with Holland/ Dozier/ Holland's 'Can I Get A Witness', as well as room for a Jagger/Richards original, 'Tell Me (You're Coming Back)'. The album hit the number 1 spot and stayed on the UK charts for nigh on twelve months.

First US Visit

Having hardly had a day off since the turn of the year, The Rolling Stones touched down at JFK on June 1 to a tumultuous reception from more than 500 screaming fans. Following a day of promotional commitments the band switched to the West Coast to appear on Dean Martin's *Hollywood Palace* TV show and to kick off their first US tour in San Bernardino a couple of days later.

By and large, apart from a couple of the dates, the tour was not well attended but the wild reaction of those who did attend, the hysterical press coverage and the famous comment of a 'refreshed' Dean Martin, "Their hair isn't long; it's just smaller foreheads and higher eyebrows", all combined to set the band up for a second onslaught later in the year.

JUNE 26, 1964
Single: It's All Over Now/Good Times Bad Times
(Decca F 11934)

Recorded at the legendary Chess Studios in Chicago on June 10 and 11, this brilliant cover of Bobby and Shirley Womack's original hit for The Valentinos was the band's first number 1 single in the UK. The B-side is an early Jagger/Richards original. The band were even visited in the studio by two of their idols, Muddy Waters and Chuck Berry.

Right: The Barron Knights support the Stones at a concert at the Bournemouth Gaumont in 1964.

Below: Fan hysteria hits New York, 1964.

Back in the UK after their American adventure, the band recorded an infamous TV appearance on *Juke Box Jury*, a weekly national TV show for the BBC regularly attracting more than 12 million viewers, which would add to the band's growing notoriety. The show's format involved the panel (the five Stones) listening to five new single releases and then judging whether the songs would be 'hits or misses'. True to form, the band voted most of the eight songs that they were forced to endure 'misses'. They even slated Elvis for being dated. The following day, the national press had a field day.

AUGUST 14, 1964
Five By Five EP (Decca DFE 8590)

If You Need Me/Empty Heart/2120 South Michigan Avenue/ Confessin' The Blues/Around and Around

Recorded in Chicago at the same time as 'It's All Over Now', 'Five By Five' includes their own homage to the legendary Chess studio in '2120 South Michigan Avenue' as well as one of their finest ever covers, a raucous re-reading of Chuck Berry's 'Around and Around'.

NOVEMBER 13, 1964
Single: Little Red Rooster/Off The Hook (Decca F 12014)

The decision to go with Willie Dixon's slow-bluesy 'Little Red Rooster', as a follow-up to the massively successful 'It's All Over Now' was a daring if not reckless move, but by this time the Stones were unstoppable. Just like its predecessor it hit the number 1 spot in no time at all.

1965: WE PISS ANYWHERE, MAN

Following three dates in Ireland, a show at the Commodore Theatre in Hammersmith and then a whistle-stop trip to RCA studios in Hollywood, where they recorded 'The Last Time', the Stones then flew to Sydney for their first foray Down Under. Having already scored nine hit singles in Australia, the fans and local media went crazy for the band. They were met by 3,000 fans at the airport and over the course of 34 dates in Australia and New Zealand played to more than 100,000 people.

JANUARY 30, 1965

The Rolling Stones No. 2 (Decca LK 4661)

Everybody Needs Somebody To Love/Down Home Girl/You Can't Catch Me/Time Is On My Side/What A Shame/Grown Up Wrong/Down The Road Apiece/ Under The Boardwalk/I Can't Be Satisfied/Pain In My Heart/Off The Hook/Susie Q

The Stones' sophomore album carried on where their debut left off. This time however, with a slew of British bands following in their wake and copping a number of older, well-known American blues and R'n'B numbers for themselves, the Stones had to be a little cuter with their approach to finding suitable songs. So they mixed it up; Solomon Burke's 'Everybody Needs Somebody To Love', was plundered almost as soon as it had been released, as were Irma Thomas's 'Time Is On My Side', Otis Redding's 'Pain In My Heart', and The Drifters' 'Under The Boardwalk', while Chuck Berry's 'You Can't Catch Me' dated from 1956 and Dale Hawkins' 'Suzie Q' from 1957.

By now the Jagger/Richard songwriting partnership was also beginning to bear fruit and 'Off The Hook' was one of their best efforts to date.

FEBRUARY 26, 1965

Single: The Last Time/Play With Fire (Decca F12104)

When Andrew Loog Oldham allegedly locked Mick and Keith in a room and threatened not to let them out until they'd written a hit single, even he couldn't have dreamed they would come up with something quite as good as this. The first A-side from the pens of Jagger/Richards, 'The Last Time' set the benchmark for a string of hit singles to follow as Mick and Keith's songwriting partnership really hit its stride. Another number 1 single and another triumph!

Right: "Bravo presents the sensation of the loudest band in the world – The Rolling Stones" or words to that effect...

Above: Far from the madding crowd – Brian, Mick and Charlie take a quiet stroll on the beach during the band's first Australian tour.

On March 18 there was an incident which was subsequently writ large in Stones folklore and serves to show how outraged the general populus was by the band around this time. Returning from their last tour show at the ABC in Romford, Bill Wyman's legendary weak bladder caused him to be 'caught short'. Stopping at a service station in Stratford, Wyman innocently asked if he could use the toilet. So offended was a certain Charles Keeley by these 'shaggy-haired monsters', that he told Bill and Mick in no uncertain terms to 'get lost', at which point Wyman allegedly walked across the road to urinate against a wall, telling Mr. Keeley, "We piss anywhere, man." National outrage ensued with Bill, Mick and Brian being fined the princely sum of £3 each for insulting behaviour.

JUNE 11, 1965

EP: Got Live If You Want It! (Decca DFE 8620)

We Want The Stones/Everybody Needs Somebody To Love/
Pain In My Heart/Route 66/I'm Moving On/I'm Alright

A scream-fest of a live recording, taped on the band's March
tour of that year.

AUGUST 20, 1965

**Single: (I Can't Get No) Satisfaction/The Spider And
The Fly** (Decca F1220)

One of the definitive Stones songs, 'Satisfaction' was recorded
at Chess Studios in Chicago during the middle of a marathon
session in early May of that year, smack-bang in the middle of a
US tour. Keith maintains that he dreamed of the riff, hastily woke
up and recorded it on a cassette player and then drifted back to
sleep. When he eventually woke the next day he discovered the
tape in the machine with a couple of minutes of acoustic strumming
followed by 40 minutes of snoring!

'Satisfaction' was the first Stones single to top the charts on both
sides of the Atlantic.

Above: The French release of
'Satisfaction' – a four-track EP with a
picture of the band braving the traffic
on the Champs-Elysees.

Right: Performing live in '65!

Left: two very different styles of
manager – the abrasive Allen Klein and
the evasive Andrew Loog Oldham.

SEPTEMBER 6, 1965

Out Of Our Heads (Decca SKL 4733)

She Said Yeah/Mercy, Mercy/Hitch Hike/That's How Strong My
Love Is/Good Times/Gotta Get Away/Talkin' 'Bout You/Cry To Me/
Oh Baby (We Got A Good Thing Going)/Heart Of Stone/The Under
Assistant West Coast Promotion Man/I'm Free

The Stones' third album in just under 18 months, and the first
wholly recorded in the US, is a bit of a step up from the first two,
with the recording, the technical proficiency of the band and
Mick and Keith's song writing all showing marked improvements.
Although produced by Andrew Loog Oldham, it's safe to assume
that legendary American engineers Dave Hassinger and Ron Malo
had a bigger influence on the sound of this record. It's tighter and
punchier all round than its predecessors and again showcases the
band's impeccable taste when it came to mining contemporary
black American music for suitable covers. However, the band this
time featured four original compositions on the album and it shows
how far they'd progressed in such a short time that they had the
confidence to do so. The killer here is 'Heart Of Stone', a brooding
ballad many thought was an obscure Southern soul song.

OCTOBER 22, 1965

**Single: Get Off Of My Cloud/
The Singer Not The Song** (Decca F 12263)

Another bona-fide classic and a worthy
follow-up to 'Satisfaction', although
strangely Keith claimed he never liked it,
that it was rushed and one of Andrew Loog
Oldham's 'worst productions'. Others were
more convinced, though; Nick Cohn, that
doyen of rock journalists, felt it captured
the spirit of the Sixties just as much as
'Blue Suede Shoes' had that of the
Fifties. The British record-buying public
concurred and 'Get Off Of My Cloud'
followed its predecessor straight to the
top of the charts.

1966: COULD YOU WALK ON THE WATER?

A story broke in the *New Musical Express* at the beginning of 1966 to the effect that the imminent new Stones long-player was to be entitled, *Could You Walk On The Water?*. The new album was to feature on its cover a photograph of a reservoir with just the Stones' heads sticking out above the water. As it transpired, this was another of Andrew Loog Oldham's brilliant hoaxes. It did, however, wind up the stuffed shirts at their label, Decca, a treat. A spokesman for the label was quoted as saying, "We would not issue it with that title for any price!"

After an almost unbroken 18 months of touring, recording and promotion the Stones were showing signs of wear and tear and were obviously in desperate need of a break. However, there were further tours of Europe and Australia to fulfil before the release of their fourth UK album, *Aftermath*.

FEBRUARY 4, 1966

Single: 19th Nervous Breakdown/As Tears Go By

(Decca F 12331)

Perhaps this was inspired by the band being literally being at the end of their tether but Mick, as ever, was coy about the song's true meaning ("It's not about anything. It's just about a neurotic bird, that's all"), although Marianne Faithfull claimed Mick wrote the lyrics after dropping acid with his then-girlfriend Chrissie Shrimpton. The B-side was a rare tender moment in the Stones' oeuvre at that time and had been written for – and a hit for – Marianne a year earlier.

Right: Dedicated followers of fashion? A group shot from 1965.

Below: A personalized note from The Rolling Stones Fan Club, including signatures from each band member and (allegedly) some of Bill Wyman's hair!

APRIL 15, 1966:

Aftermath (Decca SKL 4786)

Mother's Little Helper/Stupid Girl/Lady Jane/Under My Thumb/Dontcha Bother Me/Goin' Home/Flight 505/High And Dry/Out Of Time/It's Not Easy/I Am Waiting/Take It Or Leave It/Think/What To Do

It's truly remarkable that after such a hectic itinerary the Stones managed to come up with this, their most accomplished work to date. However, at this point in the Sixties, pop writing was reaching new creative highs with The Beatles' *Rubber Soul*, Dylan's *Highway 61 Revisited* and The Beach Boys' masterwork, *Pet Sounds*, and the Stones weren't about to be left behind. This, their first album of self-penned songs, is underrated in the great canon of pop music and sees the band pushing the boundaries in their songwriting, instrumentation and arrangements. As well as being an extremely gifted guitarist, Brian Jones was now developing into a multi-talented musician, as illustrated by his playing of such varied instruments as the harmonica, dulcimer, marimba and harpsichord. However, as the engineer Dave Hassinger noted, the band were becoming increasingly dysfunctional. Mick and Keith's songwriting inevitably drew them closer together, with Andrew frequently encouraging and cajoling them. The more taciturn and stoical Watts and Wyman formed their own partnership, that of being one of the tightest rhythm sections around, and this left Brian somewhat out on a limb.

Although he felt increasingly isolated both during the recording process and while the band were on the road Brian, possibly bolstered by his burgeoning relationship with Italian actress and model Anita Pallenberg, was (when he bothered to turn up) flourishing in the studio. His playing graces *Aftermath*, the dulcimer on 'Lady Jane' being particularly exquisite and the marimbas on the magnificent 'Under My Thumb' underpin the chugging guitars and drums perfectly.

There are many great moments on *Aftermath*, from the opening salvo of 'Mother's Little Helper' ("What a drag it is getting old"), through 'Lady Jane', 'Under My Thumb' (a number 1 hit for Chris Farlow), 'Flight 505' and 'Out Of Time' to the closer 'What To Do', a paean

to on-the-road boredom. However, the *pièce de résistance* here is the epic eleven-minute jam that closes Side One of the original vinyl album, 'Goin' Home'. Featuring Ian Stewart on piano, the song starts conventionally enough but from about three minutes mutates into a thrilling wig-out. At the time it truly broke the mould and paved the way for the band's later move into the rock firmament.

MAY 13, 1966

Single: Paint It Black/Long Long While (Decca F 12395)

Aptly described at the time by the magazine *Melody Maker* as 'a glorious Indian raga-rock riot', 'Paint It, Black' apparently started as a piss-take of the band's former business manager, Eric Easton. Bill was messing about on the Hammond organ aping Eric, who had once played professionally, when Charlie picked up the rhythm and Brian picked out the melody on a newly-acquired sitar.

John Lennon accused the Stones of flagrantly copying The Beatles, who had employed the sitar on 'Norwegian Wood' a few months earlier. This irked Brian in particular, who stated: "What utter rubbish. You might as well say that we copy all the other groups by playing guitar."

A number 1 smash on both sides of the Atlantic.

SEPTEMBER 13, 1966

Single: Have You Seen Your Mother, Baby, Standing In The Shadow?/Who's Driving Your Plane (Decca F12497)

The first Rolling Stones single to be released simultaneously in the UK and US, this was expected to hit the top spot in the charts but floundered, eventually reaching number 5 in the UK and number 9 in the US. Perhaps it was due to the rather muddled production on the record. Keith maintains to this day that it was released in a hurry and, with hindsight, a bit more work would have polished it up to great effect.

Or perhaps it was the sight of the Stones dressed in drag for the promotional campaign for the single that put people off? Certainly the famous picture of the band and the accompanying film clip are hilarious, if not particularly alluring.

Above: Brian, Mick and Charlie on set for yet another television appearance.

Left: The UK cover for *Aftermath*, released April 1966.

1967: ARRESTING TIMES

JANUARY 20, 1967

Between The Buttons (Decca SKL 4582)

Yesterday's Papers/My Obsession/Back Street Girl/Connection/
She Smiled Sweetly/Cool, Calm And Collected/All Sold Out/
Please Go Home/Who's Been Sleeping Here?/Complicated/Miss
Amanda Jones/Something Happened To Me Yesterday

Between The Buttons is a curio of an album which divided opinion
as much today as it did on its release. It's certainly the band's most
English-sounding record, both lyrically and compositionally. Eminent
rock critic Roy Carr said that, 'Back Street Girl' and 'Connection'
apart, it sound sounded like a bunch of vaudevillean Kinks outtakes.
Other critics were kinder, the *Toronto Star* writing, "They have that
one quality which sets The Stones in a category all their own: a
strong personal contact with the listener. Unlike The Beatles, who
touch mainly the mind, the Stones touch the emotions and the gut."

It was the last Stones album Andrew Loog Oldham would have a
hand in producing. It seems at this point in the story his influence was
beginning to wane and certainly his ambitions to be the English Phil
Spector were annoying and frustrating the band. The shadow of Allen
Klein, the band's all-powerful US business manager, was looming
large and Andrew would soon be ousted. However, the release of the
album was soon to be overshadowed by more serious events.

JANUARY 13, 1967

Single: Let's Spend The Night Together/Ruby Tuesday

(Decca F 12546)

It all seems faintly ridiculous now, but at the start of 1967 the Stones
were firmly established as enemies of the state, both in the UK and
the US, and the release of 'Let's Spend The Night Together', only
served to enflame the situation and enhance their notoriety.

So outraged were the bastions of morality, particularly in America,
that Ed Sullivan famously had to beg Mick to change the lyrics to
"Let's spend some time together" when the band performed the
song on his coast-to-coast networked TV show. Although the single
was not officially banned in the US many radio stations played the
B-side, 'Ruby Tuesday' instead.

The band further stoked the fires of indignation when they
appeared on the family variety TV show *Sunday Night At The London
Palladium* to promote the single. Traditionally, each act which had
appeared would stand waving at the audience on a revolving stage at
the show's denouement. The Stones, irked by the sound production
on the show, flatly refused, leading to an extremely heated argument
between Mick and Andrew Loog Oldham.

Above: Fans get their message across.

Above Right: Brian attends the Monterey Pop Festival, June 1967.

Right: Psychedelia kicks in, one of a number of famous shots by
the late Michael Cooper.

AUGUST 18, 1967
Single: We Love You/Dandelion (Decca F 12654)

The ominous sounds of echoing footsteps, dragging chains and the slamming of a cell door kick off the Stones' most psychedelic offering to date. Recorded soon after the Appeal Court in London had quashed Mick and Keith's drug convictions, this was a commercial failure (only reaching number 8 in the UK chart) but an artistic milestone. With Nicky Hopkins on piano, Brian on mellotron and (allegedly) Lennon and McCartney on backing vocals, 'We Love You', is a magnificent evocation of the period. The lyrics were apparently penned on prison notepaper by Mick while he was awaiting trial in Brixton jail.

SEC. ROW SEAT
92 J 12
W E S T
Retain Stub — Good Only
TUES.
8:00 P.M. JUNE 17
Davis Printing Limited
THE ROLLING STONES
PRICE-7.27+RST .73-$8.00
ADMIT ONE. Entrance by Main Door or by West Door, Carlton St.
Maple Leaf Gardens
LIMITED
CONDITION OF SALE: Upon refunding the purchase price the management...

Right: Maple Leaf Gardens ticket, Toronto. June 1975.

Below: Ultimate rock chick chic – Marianne Faithfull and Anita Pallenberg.

Redlands Bust – Who Breaks A Butterfly On A Wheel?

On February 12, fifteen police officers raided a party at Keith's country residence, Redlands, in West Wittering in West Sussex. Various illegal substances were found on the premises and both Mick and Keith were taken away for questioning.

On the day Mick and Keith appeared in court, May 10, to be granted bail of £100 each, Brian was also arrested at his London flat and charged with unlawful possession of drugs. He was subsequently granted bail in the sum of £250. The UK establishment's hunting down of the Stones was now in full force.

On June 27, at Chichester Crown Court, Mick was found guilty of illegal possession of two drugs. Keith was found guilty the following day of allowing hemp to be smoked at his residence. Following a night in the cells in Brixton jail for Mick and a similar incarceration in Wormwood Scrubs for Keith, the pair were sentenced at Chichester the next day.

What followed were draconian sentences: Mick jailed for three months and ordered to pay £100 costs, Keith handed a whopping 12-month sentence with £500 costs. Their friend, London art dealer Robert Fraser, was given six months and £200 costs. Freed pending their appeal, the High Court granted the pair bail for the then-astronomical sum of £7,000 each.

Perhaps the most astonishing aspect of the whole episode occurred when *The Times*, arguably the UK's most pro-establishment newspaper, took the unprecedented step of devoting a page of editorial in its leader column to the plight of Mick and Keith.

Famously headlined 'Who Breaks A Butterfly On A Wheel?', the editorial was written by the paper's editor William Rees-Mogg and within it, he compared the drugs Mick had been charged with possessing to those that the Archbishop of Canterbury had bought at Rome airport after a visit to the Vatican. He essentially rubbished the case against Mick, arguing that the media and public furore which had followed their arrest was completely unjustified and that Mick was the victim of a witch-hunt. He appealed for common sense, and ultimately common sense prevailed when the cases against Mick and Keith were quashed on appeal.

1968: ALL CHANGE

1968 can be seen as a pivotal year for the Stones. With the band off the road and uncertain of their future, they decamped to the studio with new producer Jimmy Miller in attempt to rediscover their collective mojo. On May 12 the band played their first UK concert appearance in two years as surprise guests at the *NME* poll-winners' concert at the Wembley Empire Pool.

DECEMBER 8, 1967:

Their Satanic Majesties Request (Decca TXS 103)
Sing This All Together/Citadel/In Another Land/2000 Man/Sing This Altogether (See What Happens)/She's A Rainbow/The Lantern/Gomper/2000 Light Years From Home/On With The Show

Universally misunderstood and rubbished on its release, *Satanic Majesties* has weathered the years well and now stands up well to re-evaluation. No matter what your personal opinion is, it cannot be denied that this is by far the most musically inventive and intriguing album in the Stones' canon. It might have been seen as a monumental error of judgement for them to go down the psychedelia road, but it was probably difficult not to get caught up in the spirit of the times, particularly with the amount of LSD doing the rounds. However, the Stones never did anything by halves and, no matter how dysfunctional they were becoming, they were never less than totally professional when it came to recording.

Andrew Loog Oldham's departure meant that for the most part *Satanic Majesties* was recorded without him. Instead, the band produced it themselves with Glyn Johns assisting on engineering duties, and without Andrew's heavy-handedness they let rip.

The music itself is a cornucopia of styles, weaving between straight-ahead psychedelic rock ('Citadel'), music-hall ('On With The Show'), pastoral whimsy ('She's A Rainbow') and acid-drenched soundscapes ('The Lantern' and 'Gomper'). In addition there's the spaced-out glory of Jagger's ode to the man of the future, '2000 Man', and Bill Wyman's haunting 'In Another Land' – a single Stateside and his only solo composition to ever feature on a bona-fide Stones album.

In relative terms, although it hit number three in the album charts, it was a commercial and critical failure. The following year the Stones would go back to basics and come roaring back.

Below: Recording 'Sympathy For The Devil', for Jean Luc Godard's *One Plus One*.

MAY 24: SINGLE:

Jumpin' Jack Flash/Child Of The Moon (Decca F 12782)

'Jumpin' Jack Flash' was a stunning riposte to those who thought the Stones were washed up after the trials and tribulations of the previous 12 months.

Birthed during rehearsals at which, initially, only Bill, Brian and Charlie were present, with Bill playing a crude riff on the organ, the song began to take shape when Mick and Keith belatedly showed up. Keith was now becoming something of an expert on obscure blues guitar tunings and the now familiar chiming riff that open the song was played on a Gibson Hummingbird tuned to an open E. Keith then double-tracked another acoustic guitar, this time played country-style, and output the results through a primitive Philips cassette recorder's extension speaker. All this, along with one of Mick's most demonic vocals to date, a booming, doom-laden bass-line, Bill Wyman's gothic organ, driving drums and Jimmy Miller's taut production, combine to make this one of the band's quintessential recordings.

The B-side, 'Child of the Moon', is a 'lost' Stones classic, a song Brian apparently wanted as the A-side.

DECEMBER 5:

Beggars Banquet (Decca SKL 4955)

Sympathy For The Devil/No Expectations/Dear Doctor/Parachute Woman/Jigsaw Puzzle/Street Fighting Man/Prodigal Son/Stray Cat Blues/Factory Girl/Salt Of The Earth

That one of the finest albums of the Sixties was delayed by nearly six months due to a dispute over its cover art stands as testament to the prudish attitudes of the times, particularly of those at the Stones' label, Decca. Recorded on and off at Olympic Studios in Barnes, West London, from early March through June 1968, the album was originally scheduled for a late summer release, but when executives at Decca saw the proposed cover art (a heavily graffitied toilet wall, inspired by a picture by American photographer Barry Fenstein) they balked and refused to sanction it. Compromises were suggested and rejected – Mick even proposed that the album be shipped in a brown paper bag with the legend 'Unfit for children' stamped on it – until finally, with both parties anxious to get the album in the market-place for Christmas, the eventual 'invitation' sleeve was agreed upon.

While the impasse was at its height, 'Street Fighting Man' was released as a single in the US with a sleeve depicting some cops putting the boot into a protester (see page 23). The sleeve was hastily withdrawn and the song banned on radio in many states for 'being subversive'. When it was finally released, the album received an almost unanimous thumbs-up. The Stones' return to their blues and rock roots was a triumph and had yielded their strongest suite of songs to date.

ANDREW LOOG OLDHAM

There is little doubt that Andrew Loog Oldham was the catalyst who made stars of The Rolling Stones. Born in Paddington, West London, in 1944 and public school-educated, he had an innate feel for publicity and from day one helped develop and foster a bad boy persona for the band which the media, looking for an alternative to those 'nice' Beatles, lapped up.

Without him they would have probably been just another young R&B band, albeit a very good one. With him, they became anti-establishment rogues, a mixture of youthful rebellion and licentious sexuality. He coined the phrase, "The Rolling Stones are more than just a group; they are a way of life." He also encouraged the nascent songwriting partnership of Mick and Keith, allegedly locking them in a room and threatening not to let them out until they had written a hit song.

It was perhaps inevitable that the Stones would outgrow Andrew's scheming, and they parted amicably in September 1967.

Above: Brian gets a smacker from girlfriend Suki Potier after his conviction for possession of drugs, September 1968.

Far left: The *Beggars Banquet* launch party. Moments before the notorious food fight.

Left: A very rare piece of in-store advertising for *Beggars Banquet*.

Overleaf: *NME* Poll Winners Concert, Wembley Empire Pool – May 12, 1968.

BEGGAR'S BANQUET
THE ROLLING STONES
* SKL 4955   * LK 4955
DECCA

BRIAN JONES

Lewis Brian Hopkins Jones was born on February 28, 1942, in the spa town of Cheltenham in Gloucestershire. His parents, Lewis Blount Jones and Louisa Beatrice Jones (*née* Simmonds) originally hailed from Wales, and had two other children: Pamela, who died aged two from leukaemia, and Barbara, who was four years Brian's junior.

Brian's parents nurtured his interest in music from an early age; his father played piano and organ and led the local church choir, and his mother was a piano teacher. Brian was proficient on a number of instruments by the time he was 15 or 16, but initially his first love was the saxophone, which he'd been inspired to pick up after hearing the great American alto player Cannonball Adderley.

From his early days he was always seen as a very bright child; at school he garnered nine 'O' levels and two 'A' levels but he countered this by being fearlessly antagonistic towards authority and convention. His parents expected Brian to attend university but instead he took great delight in taking a number of menial jobs in his hometown, getting sacked from several for petty pilfering and poor time-keeping.

By the late Fifties, and now proficient on sax, piano, clarinet and guitar, he was playing with several local Cheltenham jazz combos including the Cheltone Six. His burgeoning love of the blues then led him to join a local R'n'B band called The Ramrods.

When Alexis Korner's Blues Incorporated pitched up in his home town Brian immediately won over its leader with his enthusiasm, so much so that Alexis gave Brian his address in London and invited him to come and stay. Soon Brian was playing regularly with Blues Incorporated and guesting with other outfits, including fellow-blues obsessive Paul Jones' band Thunder Odin's Big Secret, which at that time were gigging around Oxford.

However, Brian's ambition was to lead his own group and soon, courtesy of Alexis, he had won over Charlie Watts and had placed a 'Musicians wanted' ad in *Jazz News*. Before long the Rollin' Stones had been born.

Brian's fall from grace emanated from the fact that Mick (encouraged by Andrew Loog Oldham) gradually usurped him to become the leader and the focal point of the Stones. Mick's songwriting partnership with Keith relegated Brian to the role of extremely talented sideman. Brian's seeming inability to contribute his own songs and his purist tendencies – he disliked what he saw as Mick and Keith's 'pop sensibilities' – left him out on a limb, while his erratic behaviour and ever-increasing drug use meant that by 1967 he had almost become a hindrance to the rest of the band.

The arrests and court cases which followed seem to crush his spirit and when, on a well-documented trip to Morocco, Keith 'stole' Anita Pallenberg from him it was almost the proverbial straw that broke the camel's back. The events surrounding his death by drowning in his swimming pool on July 3, 1969, remain shrouded in mystery to this day. Conspiracy theories abound but with the death of a couple of key witnesses, builder Frank Thorogood in 1993 and Stones minder Tom Keylock in 2009 it seems any questions will remain unanswered.

1969

The year that ended the Sixties would prove to be a watershed for The Rolling Stones. To the impartial observer the band, after the success of *Beggars Banquet*, might have appeared to be in fine fettle. However, if you delved a little further in, it soon became apparent that things were not as rosy as they seemed. Following numerous busts the previous year, Brian in particular was in a fragile state. He had become withdrawn and elusive and his relationships with Mick and Keith had broken down almost irretrievably. The fact that Keith had absconded with Brian's 'lady', Anita Pallenberg, during a trip to Morocco in 1967 certainly hadn't helped matters. He'd been sidelined by Mick and Keith's songwriting partnership and his contributions to the band's recording sessions had dwindled dramatically. His dislike of the band's musical direction was becoming apparent and it was obvious that matters were coming to a head.

On June 9 it was announced that Brian was leaving the group. Mick, Keith and Charlie had driven to Brian's East Sussex cottage, Cotchford Farm (once owned by A A Milne), and they'd agreed reasonably amicably that it was in the band's interest that Brian leave. In anticipation, the Stones had already auditioned and enrolled a replacement the week before. On the recommendation of Ian Stewart, Mick Taylor, a 19-year-old prodigy who had been a fixture in John Mayall's Bluesbreakers, was to be the new Rolling Stone.

Above: Brian's golden age? The full, original Stones lineup in concert in 1965.

Left: Brian in happier days.

Right: Bill and Charlie were the only Stones to attend Brian's funeral.

On July 3, word came through to the band that Brian had died. The events surrounding his death have to this day largely remained a mystery. He was pulled unconscious from the swimming pool at Cotchford Farm by his girlfriend Anna Wohlin and builder Frank Thorogood. Anna, a nurse, tried reviving him but to no avail. He was dead by the time an ambulance arrived.

The rest of his erstwhile bandmates were understandably shocked and considered cancelling the free show that had been planned for Hyde Park on July 5, but decided to press ahead as a tribute to Brian: and it so it was that barely two days after the death of one of their founding members, and with new guitarist Mick Taylor making his live debut, The Rolling Stones played to an estimated crowd of more than 250,000 in London's Hyde Park. It was an understandably ramshackle affair but after Mick had read Shelley's 'Adonais' in tribute to Brian, and thousands of white butterflies had been released into the London sky, the band stormed into a version of Johnny Winter's 'I'm Yours, She's Mine' and the good vibes of a beautifully sunny summer afternoon kicked in.

1969: DEATH AND DISORDER AT ALTAMONT

Originally scheduled to take part in Golden Gate Park, San Francisco, and then at the Sears Point Raceway, the Stones' own free concert instead got moved to the less salubrious grounds of the Altamont Speedway race track, around 30 miles from Oakland, when the necessary permits were refused. Others billed to perform were Santana, The Flying Burrito Brothers, Crosby Stills Nash and Young and The Grateful Dead. The chaotic organization of the event, however, ensured it would go down in history for all the wrong reasons. Using the local Hell's Angels as a security force (as suggested by The Grateful Dead's road crew) proved a disaster. As the day wore on, with drugs and drink making the crowd and the Angels ever more fractious, beatings and fights became commonplace. At the end of the night 18-year-old Meredith Hunter had been stabbed to death in front of the stage by a member of the Hell's Angels after allegedly pulling a gun on one of their number.

Right: "Hey people, hey people ... come on, let's be cool ..."

JULY 11

Single: Honky Tonk Women/You Can't Always Get What You Want (Decca F 12952)

A tinkle on the cowbells by producer Jimmy Miller, followed by the whip-crack of Charlie's snare drum and that riff from Keith, and we're into one of The Rolling Stones' signature songs. It was to prove one of their biggest-selling singles, spending five weeks at the top of the UK charts and four weeks at number one in the US.

Following the Hyde Park show the band went their separate ways, Mick to Australia to take the starring role in the film *Ned Kelly*, Keith to be with Anita, who was to give birth to their first child, Marlon, on August 10, the others to take a break before returning to Olympic to continue work on the next album and then to start preparing for their forthcoming American tour, their first for well over three years.

The 23-show US tour would gross nearly $2 million and rewrite the rule book for superstar acts touring the US. No longer would the headline act play for 20 minutes to thousands of screaming teenagers. The Rolling Stones had grown up, and their audience with them; this time they would play for the best part of two hours and their audience would dance and listen. However, the criticism they received in some quarters, over ticket pricing and accusations that the Stones had 'sold out', would result in a tour due to wind down in the gentle climes of Florida's West Palm Beach on November 30 instead culminating in an event many felt signalled the death of the 'peace and love' era of the late Sixties: the almost apocalyptic free show that was Altamont.

DECEMBER 5

Let It Bleed (Decca SKL 5025)

Gimme Shelter/Love In Vain/Country Honk/Live With Me/Let It Bleed/Midnight Rambler/You Got The Sliver/Monkey Man/You Can't Always Get What You Want

By the time of its release, the Stones had assumed the mantle of 'the greatest rock'n'roll band in the world'. Certainly there were few who could deny this claim; The Beatles had all but split and hadn't played live for more than four years, Led Zeppelin had yet to fulfil their massive potential and The Who, undeniably a fantastic live act, could not match the Stones in terms of either record or ticket sales.

Let It Bleed had been recorded on and off over the previous 12 months or so, with the final touches (including Merry Clayton's magnificently eerie vocal on 'Gimme Shelter') being added at Elektra Studios in LA shortly before the start of the American tour.

It was essentially a truncated band which played across most of the record; Brian Jones appears nominally on percussion on 'Midnight Rambler' and on autoharp on Keith's 'You Got The Sliver', while new recruit Mick Taylor adds slide to the countrified version of Honky Tonk Women that is 'Country Honk' and guitar to 'Live With Me'. Elsewhere the band is augmented by Nicky Hopkins on piano, the ubiquitous Leon Russell and

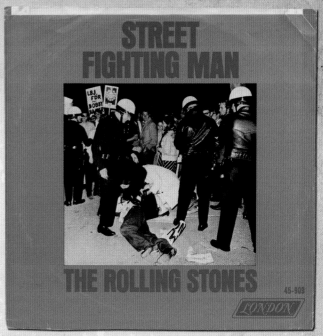

Keith's best buddy, sax player extraordinaire Bobby Keys. Al Kooper adds French horn, piano and organ to 'You Can't Always Get What You Want', while Stu tinkles the ivories on the title track. Seen by many as an era-defining album, the record certainly exudes menace and more sleaze than even *Beggars Banquet*. 'Gimme Shelter' seems to soundtrack the moment, evoking the escalating Vietnam War and the death of the Sixties dream, and 'Midnight Rambler' (a staple of the live show to this day) takes as its subject matter the infamous Boston Strangler.

Elsewhere, powered by one of Keith's most memorable riffs, the sleaze continues unabated on 'Monkey Man', a song made even more memorable as the soundtrack to that cataclysmic scene in Martin Scorsese's *Goodfellas*. Never a band to forget their roots, there is a nod to the Delta Blues with a cover of what was at the time a newly-discovered Robert Johnson side, 'Love In Vain' (written by Woody Payne), which features some lovely mandolin by Ry Cooder.

The ethereal massed voices of the London Bach Choir are the unlikeliest bedfellows you'd expect to find on a Stones album, but they segue beautifully into Keith's plaintive acoustic guitar at the beginning of the epic final track, 'You Can't Always Get What You Want', a song that Marianne Faithfull claims was written about her love affair with drugs. Sex and drugs are all over this album and it was to set the template for what was to come as the Stones swaggered into the new decade as the undisputed heavyweight champions of rock'n'roll.

Above left: With Jimmy Miller, recording *Let It Bleed*.

Above: The impossibly hard to find banned sleeve for the withdrawn US single of 'Street Fighting Man'.

Left: Live in the US, 1969.

Citation of Achievement

1969

presented by

BROADCAST MUSIC, INC.

to

KEITH RICHARDS

*in recognition of the great national popularity,
as measured by broadcast performances,
attained by*

HONKY TONK WOMEN

Edward M. Crane
PRESIDENT

Theodora Zavin
SENIOR VICE-PRESIDENT
Performing Rights Administration

"The Rolling Stones are more than just a group; they are a way of life."

Andrew Loog Oldham

Left: BMI certificate awarded to Keith Richards, 1969.

ROLLING STONES

VRIJDAGAVOND 9 OKTOBER 1970
Aanvang: 9 uur; zaal open: 7.30 uur
AMSTELHAL van het nieuwe RAI-Gebouw te
Amsterdam; ingang: Wielingestraat

Presentatie:

SBA
RADIO VERONICA
ORGANISATIEBUREAU PAUL ACKET

Prijs: f 15,— (inklusief vermakelijkhedenbelasting)

8735

№ 14252

BORA-BORA

AIR MAIL · PARAVION

See you shortly
Hope ya like
new record

Mick
† B

Photo, Edition et Copyright: Erwin Christian, Bora-Bora, Polynésie Française 41

ROLLING STONES
RECORDS
69 NEW OXFORD ST
LONDON W1
ANGLETERRE
ENGLAND

AIR MAIL PARAVION

"It's not about anything. It's just about a neurotic bird, that's all."

Mick Jagger, putting to rest the myths surrounding the lyrics of 'As Tears Go By'.

Left: Mick Jagger postcard to Rolling Stones Records office, circa 1978.

Above: Amsterdam ticket, European tour, 1970.

1970: A NEW ERA

The first year of the new decade was a relatively quiet one for The Rolling Stones. Recriminations from Altamont rumbled on – the Stones sued the Sears Point International Raceway for $4,580,000 for breach of contract and fraud and then were sued themselves by various landowners and ranchers for $375,000 for damage around Altamont itself.

Money was also becoming a major issue. On the face of it, the band should have been living the life of rock royalty, but although they'd each got a sizeable cash sum when Allen Klein negotiated a new deal with Decca it was apparent that things were not as comfortable as they seemed. The government of the time had imposed a 98% tax on the mega-rich and the band owed a fortune in back taxes. Towards the end of July the band issued a statement to the effect that their contract with Klein's ABKCO company had been terminated. The following day their contract with Decca expired.

By now plans were well afoot for The Rolling Stones to start their own label. Negotiations had been ongoing with Marshall Chess, the son of legendary Chess label co-owner Leonard, to run the new label and distribution deals were being investigated.

At the end of August the band headed out on a six-week European tour that would take them through Scandinavia to West Germany, France, Italy, Austria and the Netherlands.

SEPTEMBER 29
Get Yer Ya-Ya's Out (Decca SKL 5065)
Jumpin' Jack Flash/Carol/Stray Cat Blues/Love In Vain/Midnight Rambler/Sympathy For The Devil/Live With Me/Little Queenie/Honky Tonk Women/Street Fighting Man

There are eight bona-fide live albums in the Stones' catalogue to date – after *Love You Live* in 1975 it almost became de rigueur to release one after every mega-money-spinning tour – but if you only require one Rolling Stones live album then this is the one. Compiled from two shows recorded at New York's Madison Square Garden on November 27 and 28, and Baltimore on November 26, 1969, it captures the Stones at the height of their live powers. Some critics have even suggested that the live versions on this album surpass the studio versions.

An expanded deluxe version of the album was released in 2009 with five extra tracks: 'Prodigal Son', 'You Gotta Move', 'Under My Thumb', 'I'm Free' and 'Satisfaction'. The new version also included a separate CD of the support artistes, BB King and Ike and Tina Turner.

Cocksucker Blues
According to legend, the terms of the Stones' split with Decca obliged them to deliver one more unreleased song that could be released as a single. Knocked out fairly swiftly by Mick crooning over a simple acoustic guitar, this tale of a rent boy plying his trade around London's West End was far too lewd and crude to ever be sanctioned as an official release. It is widely available on bootlegs.

Right: Get Yer Ya's Out! – "Oh New York City, you talk a lot. Let's have a lot at ya!"

MICK TAYLOR

Michael Kevin Taylor was born on January 17, 1949, in Welwyn Garden City, Hertfordshire. He was raised in Hatfield where his father worked as a fitter at the de Havilland aircraft company.

Mick, encouraged by a young uncle, began to play guitar at the tender age of nine. He then went on to form several bands in his early to mid-teens including The Juniors and Strangers.

In 1965, when he was just 16, he went to see British blues legend John Mayall perform with his band the Bluesbreakers at The Hop in Welwyn Garden City. It was an evening that would change his life for ever. At this point in the Bluesbreakers' long and chequered history Eric Clapton held the coveted lead guitarist's gig, but this particular evening he was conspicuous by his absence. After the Bluesbreakers had played their first set, Taylor took it upon himself to ask John Mayall if he could play with the band, telling Mayall that he was a fan and knew the songs. It was an audacious move, but Mayall consented and was so impressed that the pair exchanged phone numbers at the end of the evening. A year or so later Taylor had joined the Bluesbreakers, replacing Peter Green, who had left taking two other members of Mayall's band with him, John McVie and Mick Fleetwood; they would eventually form Fleetwood Mac.

The 17-year-old Taylor was a prodigious talent. He soon became known for his virtuoso slide and lead playing and this would bring him to the attention of the Stones. Taylor would cut just one album with the Bluesbreakers, *Crusade*, but it would cement his talent on disc and earn him a slew of admirers among his contemporaries.

By the time the Stones were ensconced in Olympic Studios recording 'Honky Tonk Women', they had recognized that Brian Jones was a spent force and that his ongoing drug problems would prevent him entering the US, thus endangering any plans to tour there. It was then that Ian Stewart suggested to the band that Mick Taylor would be the ideal replacement for Brian.

Taylor would go on to grace the Stones' recordings and live shows until his departure in December 1974, disgruntled by the lack of writing credits he felt were due but not delivered and worn out by increasing drug problems.

There's no doubt that Taylor's tenure with the band was a wonderfully productive time. Taylor's playing certainly up the ante and perfectly dove-tailed with Keith's style of riffing.

Following his departure from the Stones, Taylor formed a short-lived band with Jack Bruce and Carla Bley. An eponymous solo album was released by CBS in 1977 and Mick mainly survived doing high-profile session work. It was at Mick Jagger's behest that Taylor contributed guitar overdubs to the expanded version of *Exile On Main Street* which finally saw the light of day in 2010.

1971: TAXILED

The UK's draconian tax regime for high earners forced the Stones' hands and a decision was made that would effectively make them rock'n'roll's first tax exiles. Their new financial advisor, Prince Rupert Lowenstein, had brought their monetary woes into sharp focus and suggested that the band take a year out of the UK, away from the long arm of the taxman. So it was that at the beginning of April the individual members began to decamp to the warm climes of the French Riviera to begin their new lives.

Prior to this, as a 'farewell' to their fans, they toured the UK for the first time in nearly five years with a short nine-date jaunt, with two shows on most nights, making 16 in all.

APRIL 16

Single - Brown Sugar/Bitch/Let It Rock (Rolling Stones Records RS 19100)

The Stones launched their own Rolling Stones label with a killer single that would preview their up-and-coming album in some style. Lyrically dubious the song might be (originally it was called 'Black Pussy'), but it is unarguably the Stones at their raunchy best. The song dated as far back as the sessions at Muscle Shoals Sound Studios in Alabama which preceded Altamont and it has that unmistakeable Southern sheen on it – although a cracking version featuring Eric Clapton on slide guitar, recorded later at Olympic on the occasion of Keith's birthday, also exists and has been much bootlegged over the years.

Previous page: Farewell to the UK (for now), live March 1971.

Below: With Atlantic Records founder, Ahmet Ertegun.

Above: Live at London's Roundhouse, March 14, 1971. Keith: the epitome of rock'n'roll.

Above: Bill: a study in concentration ...

Above: ... and Mick giving his all.

APRIL 23

Sticky Fingers (Rolling Stones Records COC 59100)

Brown Sugar/Sway/Wild Horses/Can't You Hear Me Knocking/
You Gotta Move/Bitch/I Got The Blues/Sister Morphine/Dead
Flowers/Moonlight Mile

Circumstances contrived to make the gestation of *Sticky Fingers* a long-drawn-out affair: but with the band out of their contract with Decca, free of Allen Klein's heavy hand and in charge of their own destiny, they could pretty much do as they pleased. Having just inked a lucrative deal with Atlantic Records boss Ahmet Ertegun, which gave Kinney (later Warner Communications) exclusive worldwide rights to Rolling Stones records, they were loosely committed to delivering six new albums in the next four years; however, in reality such was the band's commercial power at this time that they could if they wished pad the deal out with compilations and solo releases.

Because of this, the Stones had slipped into a new way of working that had evolved over the last couple of years or so. Studios seemed to be booked on an ad hoc basis whenever there was the time or a splurge of creativity; unfinished songs were left in the can to be polished up later or discarded for ever, and then when the time was right and there was enough material to fill two sides of a long-player, overdubs and finishing touches would complete the album-making process: and so *Sticky Fingers* came together over a period of around 14 months. Three songs – 'Brown Sugar', Mississippi Fred McDowell's 'You Gotta Move', and 'Wild Horses' – were initially laid down at the famous Muscle Shoals Sound Studio in Alabama in December 1969 before the fateful Altamont free show. The low-down Southern sound they managed to capture in a hectic three days of recording would set the template for the album as a whole.

Back in England in mid-December work continued, on and off at Olympic and, utilizing the band's brand-new mobile recording facility at Mick's house, Stargroves in Newbury, Berkshire, right through April 1971. What emerged was the band's dirtiest, most salacious-sounding album to date. Drug references abound, what with 'head full of snow' (Moonlight Mile), 'sweet cousin cocaine' (Sister Morphine), and 'cocaine eyes' (Can't You Hear Me Knocking'). Even 'Brown Sugar' was perhaps misconstrued as being a reference to Mexican heroin: but if illegal substances were rife, they weren't dulling the band's musical ingenuity. With Mick Taylor now fully bedded in they were firing on all cylinders. The guitar interplay and Bobby Key's masterful sax on 'Can't You Hear Me Knocking' can make the hairs stand up on the back of your neck: and when they rock, they rock. This is all killer with absolutely no filler. Right from the off the album blasts into focus with 'Brown Sugar', straight into 'Sway' before a softly strummed acoustic guitar heralds the sad, wistful 'Wild Horses', Mick's ode to Marianne Faithfull. Following the aforementioned epic 'Can't You Hear Me Knocking' they slow it down with the mournful 'You Gotta Move' featuring Mick Taylor's sublime slide guitar. Side Two is a more subdued affair; 'Bitch' romps along powered by another of Keith's trademark licks and Bobby Keys' pumping, rasping sax, 'I Got The Blues' does exactly what you'd expect before 'Sister Morphine' – a harrowing paean to addiction co-written and originally recorded by Marianne Faithfull – quietens things down again. Finally we get a decadent country lilt through 'Dead Flowers' and the closer, the majestic,

haunting 'Moonlight Mile'. All this and one of the most famous and controversial sleeves in rock'n'roll history, designed by Andy Warhol and reputedly costing £15,000 (a fortune in those days).

Astonishingly, especially now that *Sticky Fingers* is regarded as one of The Rolling Stones' finest albums – if not the finest album – of their career to date, at the time of its release it was not universally well regarded. *Rolling Stone*'s high-minded critic Greil Marcus, whilst digging the music, railed against what he saw as racist and sexist lyrics (particularly on 'Brown Sugar') and the overt drug references that litter the album.

Right: *Sticky Fingers* photo shoot. Who's holding up Mick Taylor's album sleeve?

1972: AROUND THE WORLD

Above: *Exile On Main Street* producer Jimmy Miller.

MAY 12

Exile On Main Street (Rolling Stones Records COC 69100)
Rocks Off/Rip This Joint/Shake Your Hips/Casino Boogie/ Tumbling Dice/Sweet Virginia/Torn And Frayed/Sweet Black Angel/Loving Cup/Happy/Turd On The Run/Ventilator Blues/ I Just Want To See His Face/Let It Loose/All Down The Line/Stop Breaking Down/Shine A Light/Soul Survivor

The Stones' legendary summer at Nellcôte on the Côte d'Azur will go down in the annals of rock history and has been documented at length many times; however, the sessions failed to yield anything resembling a finished album and the band, under pressure to have one ready for release ahead of a planned American tour due to start in June, again had to decamp to Sunset Sound in LA late in 1971 to tidy up a number of tracks. In reality probably only seven of the album's 18 songs ('Rip This Joint', 'Shake Your Hips', 'Casino Boogie', 'Happy', 'Rocks Off', 'Turd On The Run' and 'Ventilator Blues') had originated in the south of France and some, notably 'Sweet Virginia', 'Sweet Black Angel', 'Loving Cup' and 'Stop Breaking Down', had been started on almost 18 months before.

At the time of its release *Exile* was, if not universally panned, than certainly treated with a certain amount of scepticism. With its murky production values and its length (well over an hour) it certainly seemed a lot of music to wade through. Now, of course, all this seems faintly ridiculous and it is seen by many as the band's greatest achievement.

Above: The iconic *Exile On Main Street* sleeve designed by John Van Hemmersveld and Norman Seiff, with photographs by Robert Frank.

Right: Keith's RIAA award for 1 million dollars-worth of sales of *Exile On Main Street* in the US.

Far right: Keith, with ubiquitous fag in the south of France.

APRIL 14

Single - Tumbling Dice/Sweet Black Angel (Rolling Stones Records RS 19103)

'Tumbling Dice' was by no means an automatic choice to preview the forthcoming album. For a long time 'All Down The Line' was considered, and indeed was released as a single in the US (accompanying 'Happy') in July of that year. It is, however, a 'grower' – one of those songs that indelibly prints itself on your consciousness.

Originally entitled 'Good Time Woman', it was first committed to tape during the sessions at Stargroves in March 1971. An early take was dusted off and cleaned up and appeared on the expanded re-issue of *Exile On Main Street* in 2010.

Despite the French connection, *Exile* is probably the Stones' most American-sounding album and is seen now as almost a template for Americana, a musical term coined around 20 years after *Exile*'s release. It certainly burrows through the roots of rock'n'roll, country, blues and R'n'B.

The expanded re-release of the album in 2010 consisted of ten previously unreleased tracks, some of which had been garnished with overdubs and vocals and cleaned up; 'Loving Cup' (an early version), 'Pass The Wine (Sophia Loren)', 'I'm Not Signifying', 'Dancing In The Light', 'So Divine (Aladdin Story)', 'Soul Survivor' (an early version with a vocal by Keith), 'Following The River', 'Plundered My Soul', 'Good Time Woman' and the instrumental jam 'Title 5'. Remarkably, the album went to number 1 in the UK album chart.

1972 US Tour

The legendary North American tour which followed the release of *Exile* was immortalized not only in Robert Greenfield's epic book *S.T.P.* but then in Robert Frank's warts-and-all documentary *Cocksucker Blues*. The band were so alarmed by what the US authorities might make of Frank's finished film that to this day it has only been shown publicly on a handful of occasions.

Renowned for its tales of high jinks and debauchery, the eight-week coast-to-coast joyride would become the template for all other aspiring acts to follow – the quintessential sex, drugs and rock'n'roll tour.

The Stones' standing and the saturation marketing that had heralded the release of *Exile* meant expectation was at fever-pitch and although they had been criticized for the perceived high prices of tickets in 1969, the demand to see them was astronomical. They sold out nearly 750,000 tickets in a matter of days and could probably have shifted twice that number. The tour grossed more than $4 million from 51 shows in 30 cities, making it, at the time, the biggest money-making tour in rock history. Promoter Bill Graham labelled The Rolling Stones 'the biggest draw in the history of mankind'. On the first date 2,000 ticketless fans rioted outside the Pacific Coliseum in Vancouver, fighting with the local police and throwing firebombs and rocks.

Production values were pushing the envelope too. Chip Monck, who had made his name as the MC at Woodstock and had designed the stage and lighting rig for the festival, was brought on board to lend his expertise to the stage set-up. A huge mirror was hung above a six-panelled stage adorned with a massive painted serpent. This was augmented by the biggest lighting rig ever used by a rock band. Although this wouldn't match the gargantuan stages that would be employed on later tours, it was certainly a giant step up from what had previously been a fairly rudimentary set-up.

Wherever the kings of rock'n'roll played they were fêted by rock royalty, luminaries from film, fashion and literature and even minor royals from small European nations. The tour attracted, at various venues, Bob Dylan, Truman Capote, Jack Nicholson, Goldie Hawn, Norman Mailer and Jackie Kennedy's sister Princess Lee Radziwill, and the Stones were even invited to the Playboy mansion at the behest of Hugh Hefner.

The support slot on the tour was allocated to Stevie Wonder, and both acts' sets were recorded for a proposed live double album which, sadly, never saw the light of day.

Below: "Uptight, everything is alright" – encoring with support act Stevie Wonder, 1972 US tour.

1972–73: STILL ON THE ROAD

The North American tour of 1972 had been a resounding success, but the usual round of trouble and strife that seemed to be ever-present with The Stones at that time was to threaten the band's equilibrium before too long. Once again tax issues raised their ugly head and the band were warned they could be bankrupted if they returned to the UK for any length of time before the end of April 1973.

To add to this, Mick and Keith's American visas were due to run out and they weren't expected to be renewed without a fight, and the band were persona non grata in France, where the local police were – on account of all the activity at Nellcôte the previous summer – ready to pounce. A proposed tour of Japan in early 1973 was also in jeopardy as the Japanese authorities were withholding work visas.

So it was in Jamaica ('the only place that would have us at the time', according to Keith) that the band re-convened to start recording the follow-up to *Exile*.

By this time Keith's well-publicized drug issues were affecting the recording process, and with producer Jimmy Miller now into the hard stuff, recording became a protracted process. With few usable finished songs in the can, but with American visas reinstated, the band decamped to LA to continue the operation. During this period they played a benefit show at the behest of Mick's new wife Bianca for the victims of a catastrophic earthquake in Nicaragua, her native country.

Recording was interrupted in December when the band (minus Keith) flew to France to (successfully) clear their names. The album would eventually be finished at Olympic in London in June 1973.

In the new year the band embarked on an 11-date, 13-show tour of Australia and New Zealand, including a diversion to Hawaii for three shows, lasting into February. On their return to the UK, the trouble that seemed to follow Keith and Anita around struck again; on June 26 the pair were arrested again, this time on firearms charges, in addition to drugs. They were accused of possessing cannabis resin and, to make matters worse, Keith was charged with illegal possession of a .38 Smith & Wesson revolver. Keith would be fined the princely sum of £205 for his misdemeanours, while Anita was let off with a conditional discharge. To cap it all, tragedy was only narrowly averted when four days later Keith's house, Redlands, was severely damaged by fire; he and Anita were lucky to escape the blaze, having allegedly been completely out of it when the fire took hold.

Right: Press conference, Copenhagen, October 1973. The hectic schedule obviously got to Mick Taylor …

Left: Keith's infamous country pile, Redlands, before the fire that would see it severely damaged, 1973.

Above: Australian artist Ian MCcausland's distinctive tour poster for the New Zealand dates.

Above: "Oh yeah!" – on stage in Copenhagen.

AUGUST 20
Single: Angie/Silver Train (Rolling Stones Records RS 19105)

The release of 'Angie' to preview forthcoming album *Goats Head Soup* certainly confused critics and fans alike. Keith's ode to his young daughter was dismissed by one of their most ardent admirers, Nick Kent (in the *NME*), as 'atrocious'. The laid-back, melodic nature of the song confused everybody; this was not what was expected from 'the greatest rock'n'roll band in the world'. Where was the rock and what had happened to the roll?

The promo film that was shot to accompany the single's release certainly didn't help matters either; Keith and Mick Taylor were filmed strumming acoustically with flowers sticking out of the headstocks of their guitars. Had the Stones gone soft? However, the band had the last laugh, with 'Angie' hitting the top spot in the American *Billboard* chart and number 5 in the UK.

AUGUST 31
Goats Head Soup (Rolling Stones Records COC 59101)

Dancing With Mr D/100 Years Ago/Coming Down Again/Doo Doo Doo Doo (Heartbreaker)/Angie/Silver Train/Hide Your Love/ Winter/Can You Hear The Music/Star Star

Following an album as successful and as era-defining as *Exile On Main Street* was always going to be problematic. Add to this all the band's trials and tribulations, and Keith and producer Jimmy Miller's escalating drug problems, and you could be forgiven for thinking that *Goats Head Soup* would turn out to be an unmitigated disaster. That it's a good as it unquestionably is, and the fact that it went immediately to the number 1 spot on both sides of the Atlantic, stands as a testament to the quality of Mick and Keith's songwriting and to the band's continuing love affair with their public.

On its release it was viewed as somewhat disappointing; however, as with a number of Stones albums it has stood the test of time extremely well.

'Dancing With Mr D' is the bastard offspring of "Sympathy For The Devil' and kick-starts the album in a suitably dark fashion, whilst Keith's poignant 'Coming Down Again' is one his finest songs. 'Doo Doo Doo Doo (Heartbreaker)' a tale of New York police misdemeanours and junkiedom, was chosen as a single Stateside and is still in the live set today. The album's finest moments, though, are saved for the final three songs on Side Two. 'Winter' is a beautiful song with magnificent Mick Taylor guitar work and Nicky Hopkins on piano. 'Can You Hear The Music' is something Brian Jones in his pomp might have embellished, with its eerie psychedelic feel underscored by flutes and African percussion.

The final cut, 'Star Star' was the most controversial. Originally called 'Starfucker', it is a tribute to the groupies of this world and includes the immortal line 'giving head to Steve McQueen'. The title was amended at the personal request of Ahmet Ertegun.

The album's success was sealed with a barnstorming tour of Europe in September and October that took the band through the UK, Austria, West Germany, Switzerland, Denmark, Sweden, the Netherlands and Belgium. Again, ticket demand far outstripped supply, and in London tickets with a face value of £2.20 were selling for £40 on the burgeoning black market.

Left: A triumphant homecoming – Wembley Empire Pool, September 1973.

Below: Berne, Switzerland ticket, European tour, September 1973.

Freikarte № 160053

Good News

ROLLING STONES
& Billy Preston In Concert

Mittwoch 26. September 1973, 19.30h
Kasse & Türöffnung 18.30h
Festhalle Bern

Good News Good News Good News

№ 160053

Good News

ROLLING STONES
& Billy Preston In Concert

Mittwoch 26. September 1973, 19.30h
Kasse & Türöffnung 18.30h
Festhalle Bern

1974: TAKING CONTROL

In November 1973 the band assembled at Musicland Studios in Munich to work on the follow-up with long-term affiliate engineer Andy Johns. Jimmy Miller, who had produced the band's five previous albums, had been jettisoned as the band sought a new direction and new inspirations. The new album would be the first to be produced by Mick and Keith, the self-styled Glimmer Twins.

JULY 26
Single: It's Only Rock'n'Roll/Through The Lonely Nights
(Rolling Stones Records RS 19114)

The title track from the forthcoming album had its origins as far back as an impromptu session at Ronnie Wood's house, The Wick, in Richmond in July 1973. Demoed by Mick and Ronnie, with David Bowie on backing vocals, the song was finished off at Stargroves in April the following year. Allegedly, Ronnie's original lead guitar part was wiped by Keith, but the finished article still includes Ronnie strumming away on a 12-string acoustic. The B-side, another 'forgotten' classic Stones ballad, had originally been recorded in Jamaica at the tail-end of 1972.

Above: US tour, 1975. Mick astride the giant inflatable that was to cause more than a little controversy, particularly in the southern states.

Left: May 1, 1975 – rolling up Madison to announce the US tour in spectacular fashion.

Right: Mick and Keith, the newly christened "Glimmer Twins".

Above: At the video shoot for the 'It's Only Rock n Roll' single.

OCTOBER 18:

It's Only Rock'n'Roll (Rolling Stones Records COC 59103)

If You Can't Rock Me/Ain't Too Proud To Beg/It's Only Rock'n'Roll (But I Like It)/Till The Next Goodbye/Time Waits For No One/Luxury/Dance Little Sister/If You Really Want To Be My Friend/Short And Curlies/Fingerprint File

Prior to its release, and much to the chagrin of the Greater London Council, a massive outbreak of *It's Only Rock'n'Roll* graffiti spread across London's streets – probably one of the first instances of guerrilla marketing.

The *NME* review concluded: "Calculated brilliance it might be, but brilliance nevertheless", and it was more or less spot-on. Both Mick and Keith had celebrated their 30th birthdays in the past year and although they might not have been everyone's idea of a 30-year-old Englishman, they were certainly maturing musically. No longer coming replete with murky sound and incoherent vocals, and with the Glimmer Twins producing, the album had a sheen that set it apart from previous offerings. The Stones now seemed to take stock of what was happening around them and rather than stand aloof, were absorbing a little of the current musical climate.

Musically, the band were at the top of their game. Mick Taylor's guitar-playing is exquisite throughout, especially on the epic 'Time Waits For No One', which he co-wrote (and again was bemused when the credit was not forthcoming). His coruscating guitar licks and Nicky Hopkins' inspirational piano-playing take the song to another level entirely.

'Luxury' does cod-reggae with a New Orleans feel, and the obligatory cover version this time around is a rip-roaring version of The Temptations' 'Ain't Too Proud To Beg'. 'Till The Next Goodbye' is a fine, country-ish ballad. There is in existence a rarely-seen promo film shot by Michael Lindsay Hogg which features a more upfront mix and a particularly lascivious Jagger vocal.

'Dance Little Sister' and 'Short And Curlies', are trademark, good-time Stones rockers, as is the opening cut 'If You Can't Rock Me', which still features in the live set to this day. However, the tour de force on the album is the brooding, malevolent 'Fingerprint File', a six-and-a-half-minute dose of FBI-induced paranoia. Mick Taylor's dextrous basslines underpin a swirling mix of double-tracked wah-wah guitar, along with 'Shaft'-like synthesizer flourishes and an Indian tabla, powering the song towards an uneasy denouement with an almost whispered spoken vocal.

It's Only Rock'n'Roll would continue the band's run of number one albums in the US but peaked at number two in their home territory, and was to be the last album to feature Mick Taylor. Unhappy at his lot and frustrated with not getting the songwriting credits he felt were due him, he announced that he was leaving the band in October. His departure threw into jeopardy the band's future plans, which including hosting their own TV series, recording their next album and a planned American tour.

When the band, along with Billy Preston (who had been a fixture on keyboards on *Goats Head Soup* and *It's Only Rock'n'Roll*) met up in Rotterdam in January 1975 to start the recording process for their next album it was with the intention of auditioning a replacement for Mick Taylor along the way. Although they had no new material to peddle, a massive US tour (their biggest yet) had been pencilled in for June through August, so it was imperative that a replacement for Mick Taylor was found as soon as possible.

Although Ronnie Wood and Keith were now bosom buddies, it was by no means a foregone conclusion that Ronnie would join The Rolling Stones. A number of possible replacements were tried out including Jeff Beck, Rory Gallagher, Wayne Perkins (who had played on Bill Wyman's debut solo album *Monkey Grip*) and Harvey Mandel (Perkins and Mandel, along with Ronnie, would appear on the forthcoming album). Eventually, on April 14 a press release from Rolling Stones Records announced:

"It is confirmed by Mick Jagger that Ronnie Wood, lead guitarist with The Faces, will be accompanying The Rolling Stones when they undertake a tour of North and South America, which is due to start in June. Although this arrangement is in no way permanent, Mick says he and the rest of the Stones are looking forward to Ronnie playing with the group."

On May 1, after a few days of rehearsals, The Rolling Stones officially announced the dates for the forthcoming tour in spectacular fashion. Performing an extended version of 'Brown Sugar' aboard a flatbed truck, they drove slowly up Fifth Avenue, attracting a frenzied crowd, before jumping into waiting limousines and speeding off.

The tour kicked off with what were ostensibly two warm-up shows at Louisiana State University in Baton Rouge on June 1 and concluded at Rich Stadium in Buffalo on August 8. More than 45 shows in 26 cities were seen by more than a million fans and the tour grossed in the region of $10 million. The tour wasn't without controversy, however; one stage prop, a giant inflatable penis, caused consternation, especially in the 'Bible Belt' Southern states, and Keith, inevitably, was arrested for possession of illegal drugs and a knife. Due to the efforts of the band's lawyer, Bill Carter, the incident in Fordyce, Arkansas, was swiftly resolved and Keith was released on $5,000 bail.

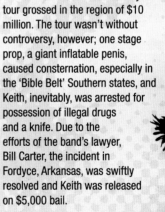

Right: The new guitarist looking somewhat sartorially challenged.

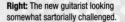

1976: CHANGE AGAIN

On December 18, 1975, Rod Stewart announced he was quitting The Faces. He was quoted as saying, "I can no longer work in a situation where the group's lead guitarist, Ron Wood, seems to be permanently on loan to The Rolling Stones." It was a get-out clause that suited both parties. In reality The Faces had splintered after the death of bass player and songwriter Ronnie Lane, and Rod's increasingly successful parallel solo career had overshadowed that of the band. On February 28, 1976, Ronnie Wood officially became a Rolling Stone.

Above: Bill Wyman takes on Atlantic Records boss Ahmet Ertegun at table tennis, backstage at Earl's Court, May 1976.

The recording process that had started almost 12 months previously in Rotterdam and continued in October and November of 1975 at Musicland in Munich and in Montreux, Switzerland, continued apace through January to the end of March. The 'audition' sessions, although fragmented, eventually yielded a pleasingly coherent body of work and one that would mark the third phase of The Rolling Stones' long career.

APRIL 20

Single: Fool To Cry/Crazy Mama (Rolling Stones Records RS 19121)
Choosing 'Fool To Cry' to preview their new album was an audacious move. In similar vein to (although more schmaltzy than) 'Angie', it divided fans and critics alike. With the band now the wrong side of 30 and the nascent punk movement about to explode it seemed that the Stones were about to abdicate their crown as the kings of rock'n'roll. In truth, 'Fool To Cry' ranks as one of the most affecting ballads The Rolling Stones have ever laid down.

APRIL 23:

Black And Blue (Rolling Stones Records COC 59106)
Hot Stuff/Hand Of Fate/Cherry Oh Baby/Memory Motel/Hey Negrita/Melody/Fool To Cry/Crazy Mama

Bill Wyman calls it about right when he states that *Black And Blue* is the least rock'n'roll album the band ever made: but all in all that's not a bad thing, for it means the band are in experimental mode, picking the ripest fruits from the musical tree of the mid-Seventies. Keith is on record as saying that because there were so many different guitarists involved in the recording process he had to be in charge, but right away you can tell that this is Mick's baby. It was his idea to bring Canned Heat's Harvey Mandel into the sessions and his lead guitar is all over the funk and grind of 'Hot Stuff', the Stones' first real foray into dance; as the B-side to 'Fool To Cry in the US' it became the band's first club hit. 'Hand Of Fate', with Wayne Perkins on guitar, is one of only two real rockers on the album, the other being the underrated 'Crazy Mama', on which Keith contributes both guitar and bass, with Ronnie making an appearance on backing vocals. 'Cherry Oh Baby' is a fairly faithful, if not particularly impressive, reworking of Eric Donaldson's Jamaican hit from 1971, and marks Ronnie Wood's first official contribution to a Stones album on guitar. The stand-out track on the album is the glorious 'Memory Motel', an epic road ballad that features a very touching dual vocal with Mick and Keith trading verses. 'Hey Negrita' is another Stones-by-numbers funk groove and 'Melody' (inspired by Billy Preston) has a nice, loose, laid-back, jazzy feel to it.

At the end of April the band kicked off a three-month European tour. As well as visiting West Germany, the UK, Belgium, the Netherlands, France, Switzerland and Austria it also took in Spain and Yugoslavia, two territories where the Stones had never played before. Overall,

the band would perform to more than half a million fans, by far their biggest European tour so far. Promoter Harvey Goldsmith claimed he'd had more than a million postal applications for the three London shows alone. Three additional dates were at added at Earls Court but they were hardly sufficient to satisfy demand and tickets prices rose dramatically on the black market. Again, they were upping the ante when it came to production values. The stage alone cost £150,000 – an astronomical sum in those days – and of course the inflatable phallus was there to shock and offend.

Shortly before the London shows, disaster nearly struck Keith (again) when he fell asleep at the wheel on the M1 and crashed his Bentley into a field near Newport Pagnell. Miraculously, although the car was a write-off, Keith emerged unscathed. However, the local boys in blue turned up some suspicious-looking substances and Keith was charged with possession (again). Tragedy struck Keith and Anita two weeks later when their baby son Tara, who was only ten months old, died of a flu virus in a Geneva hospital.

Following the tour the band had most of the rest of the summer off, but returned to the live arena on August 21 to play their biggest gig in the UK since the free Hyde Park show in 1969. At Knebworth House in rural Hertfordshire they played to an estimated crowd of around 200,000 people. Also on the bill that day were Lynyrd Skynyrd and 10CC. As was the norm in those days, the Stones were fashionably late (in this case nearly four hours) but the restless crowd were soon sated by a massive 28-song set which lasted more than two-and-a-half hours and, unusually at the time, spanned the band's entire career to date. The event was filmed and recorded, but no official film or live album has ever seen the light of day.

Below: "Woody" resplendent in obligatory shades.

Top right: Earls Court Arena, London prepares for a Rolling Stones fan invasion in May 1975.

Right: Rural Hertfordshire, Saturday, August 21, 1976, Knebworth Park. All Human life is here.

Above: Backstage guest pass sticker, European Tour, 1976.

Below: Earls Court ticket, London, May 1976.

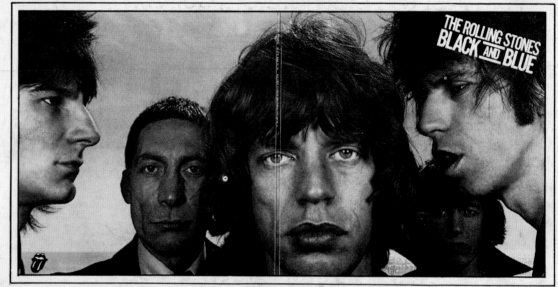

ROLLING STONES RECORDS

wea Records Limited

Single
Fool to Cry/Crazy Mama
RS 19121

THE ROLLING STONES
BLACK AND BLUE

COC 59106

EARLS COURT ARENA
(OPPOSITE WARWICK ROAD EXIT EARLS COURT TUBE STATION)

HARVEY GOLDSMITH in association with
FIVE ONE PRODUCTIONS presents

The Rolling Stones
IN CONCERT
Wednesday, May 26th, 1976
at 8-0 p.m.   (Doors open 6·30)
NO ADMISSION AFTER 8-15 p.m.

GALLERY · £2·00

FOR CONDITIONS OF SALE SEE OVER

BLOCK
77

★

B 31

TO BE RETAINED

"You're my fucking singer."

Charlie Watts' legendary response to a drunk Mick Jagger asking "where's my drummer?". Charlie ended the conversation by knocking Mick out with a left-hook.

WEA Records

Request the pleasure of your company
at a Party for

THE ROLLING STONES

at The Cockney Pride (6 Jermyn Street)
on Friday 21st May

Midnight – until everything runs out

Drinks, Pub food, Dancing, very wonderful company

**"Mick's rock;
I'm roll."**

Keith Richards

Opposite and above: WEA Records, Rolling Stones party invitation, May 1976.

DEAR ROLAND

Sorry I could not meet you. I had to leave at 10:00 AM. for Washington. However you will not have any trouble if you follow these notes.

1. I suggest you go to Vienna on the morning of June 22nd — to arrive in Vienna around 12:00 noon.

2. Go to the hotel first + tell them you would like to see the rooms they have blocked for you. I am enclosing copies of our correspondence.

    A. Try to place everyone on one floor

    B. Must have at least on security man on each floor housing a musician.

    C. Callaghan should be next to Percy Thrower

    D. Benger & Poweski near Arthur Ashe.

    E. Try to get large beds for everyone.

    F. Keep Bill Wyman away from Keith because of noise

"You will not have any trouble if you follow these notes ... Keep Bill Wyman away from Keith because of noise."

The Rolling Stones' manager

Left and opposite: A rare look at the demands placed on a manager at a Vienna hotel during the chaotic 1976 European Tour by the band's manager. Jagger had the alter-ego of tennis player Arthur Ashe while Richards' enjoyed the disguise of TV gardener Percy Thrower.

G. EVERY ONE GETS ROOMS FOR SINGLE OCCUPANCY
HOWEVER, THE HOTEL SHOUL GIVE US **LARGE** ROOMS.

H. ROOMS SPECIFIC OTHER THAN SINGLES ARE AS FOLLOWS:

(1.) PATRICK MOORE (RON WOOD) MUST HAVE **LARGE** BED

(2) OLLIE BROWN **MUST** HAVE LARGE BED.

(3) ARTHUR ASHE (MICK J.) MUST HAVE DELUXE SUITE WITH
ATTACHED LUGGAGE ROOM.

(4) JAMES BURKE (BILLY PRESTON) GETS A SUITE

(5) PETER WEST (CHARLIE WATTS) **MUST** HAVE LARGE BED.

(6) SECURITY MEN MUST BE NEAR MUSICIANS

(7) PETER RUDGE **MUST** HAVE LARGE BED.

(8) ALAN DUNN **MUST** HAVE CONNECTING DOOR WITH
JENNIE-COLLEN-SMITH.

(9) PERCY THROWER (KEITH RICHARD) GETS A SUITE.

(10) DEBBIE FREIS + BILL ZYSBLATT **MUST** HAVE
CONNECTING ROOMS.

(11) ROBIN DAY GETS A SUITE.

(12) JOHN VICTOR SHOULD BE CLOSE TO PERCY THROWER.

1977–78: STILL IN TROUBLE

Keith's misdemeanours the previous summer meant he was back in court on January 10. He maintained the jacket he had been wearing which had contained the illicit substances wasn't his and he'd grabbed it in a hurry after a show. This was backed up by Ian Stewart and the band's long-term road/tour manager and logistics director Alan Dunn. Eventually Keith was found guilty of possessing cocaine and not guilty of possessing a tiny amount of LSD. He was fined £750 and ordered to pay £250 costs. However, Keith's escalating drug use was to land him in even hotter water before too long.

In mid-February the band inked a lucrative new deal with Atlantic in the US and with EMI for the rest of the world. A double live album recorded during the last North American and European tours was to be the first release for their new paymasters. To create a point of difference from the bog-standard double album of the time, it was decided to book the tiny El Mocambo club in Toronto where the band would go back to their roots and play a heavily blues-infused set which would be recorded for the new live album.

On arrival in Toronto, though, Anita Pallenberg was stopped at Customs with 10 grams of hashish and a small quantity of heroin. The following day the Canadian police raided Keith's hotel room where they found another ounce of high-grade smack. This was serious. Both Keith and Anita had their passports confiscated. The amount of heroin they had been found in possession of was enough to mean Keith could be charged with trafficking which, if found guilty, might mean a life sentence. Even a lesser charge of possession could result in a seven-year stretch in jail. There was no doubt that Keith was now in a bad way and a serious addict. He was under virtual house arrest at his hotel and in order for him to be able to function, other people had to buy drugs for him.

The club show went ahead as planned, and although ragged, the band rescued enough good material to fill one side of the proposed double album, but now there was a genuine fear that Keith would receive a lengthy jail sentence and there were questions about the Stones' future. Could they continue without him?

A Free Keith campaign now kicked in, with several fans staging a vigil outside Keith's hotel and then outside the courthouse. Anita's case went to trial on March 14 and she got off with two nominal fines. Keith's trial was set for June 27. Behind the scenes, the band's lawyers were working on how to keep Keith out of jail, while various members of the camp were trying to find a way to wean him off heroin.

Eventually, a reputable clinic was found in New Jersey and subsequently, the court case was adjourned until the beginning of December. The live album, entitled *Love You Live* and complete with a particularly salacious cover designed by Andy Warhol, was eventually released on September 23 and hit the Top 5 in both the UK and the US.

With Keith's addiction and court case hanging over him, the best thing for the band to do was to try and do what they do best and to get him to concentrate on making some music. With this in mind they relocated to EMI's Pathé Marconi studios in Paris to commence work on their new album. The sessions continued on and off until March and were some of the most productive of the band's career. Around 50 songs were started and the band, minus Mick and Bill Wyman, even had time to record a festive single for Keith – a version of Chuck Berry's 'Run Rudolph Run' which, coupled with a cover of Toots and the Maytals' 'Pressure Drop', was released in December 1978.

Top: Buffalo gig guest pass.

Above: Video shoot for 'Miss You'.

Right: Mick with Andy Warhol at the *Love You Live* launch party.

Below right: The extremely rare US single sleeve for 'Beast of Burden'.

Below: New York City, May 1978. Group shot by Michael Putland.

Overleaf: Extremely rare in-store promotional poster for *Some Girls*, 1978.

MAY 19

Single: Miss You/Far Away Eyes (Rolling Stones Records EMI 2802)

One of the most successful Stones singles ever and a masterpiece in terms of timing and of its execution, 'Miss You' proved that the Stones hadn't let the grass grow under their feet and when it came to making contemporary-sounding records they were still as good as anyone. With Mick now firmly ensconced with Jerry Hall, the New York club scene had become the pair's playground. Disco was at its zenith and 'Miss You' was the perfect embodiment of a rock'n'roll band making dance music. An extended version was released on pink vinyl and gave the Stones their first US number 1 single for more than five years.

JUNE 16:

Some Girls (Rolling Stones Records CUN 39108)

Miss You/When The Whip Comes Down/ Just My Imagination/Some Girls/Lies Respectable/Before They Make Me Run/ Beast Of Burden/Shattered

By any standard, *Some Girls* is a remarkable body of work. Keith's travails, the punk, New Wave and disco explosions of the previous 18 months or so and many critics' perception that the band had passed their sell-by date all served to give the Stones the impetus they needed to prove to the world they were still relevant and could compete (and beat) the many would-be usurpers of their crown. Fiery, funny and funky in equal measure, it manages to be contemporary, eclectic, self-effacing and controversial. Aside from disco with 'Miss You', there is the punkiness of 'When The Whip Comes Down', 'Shattered' and 'Respectable', the hilarious faux-country of 'Far Away Eyes' and the pop-soul cover of the Temptations' 'Just My Imagination'. Add to this Keith's superb, self-mythologizing 'Before They Make Me Run' and you have what many consider to be the last great Rolling Stones album.

NEW ALBUM
THE ROLLI
100% MIRACLE FIBRE
BEAUTIFUL YOU
in a few seconds
Som
STYLE No. SK-109
Some Girls
6 WIGS in ONE
FarAwayEyes
Laughter, joy, and loneliness
and sex and sex and sex and sex
CAPLESS
BEAU C

Above: Extremely rare in-store promotional poster for *Some Girls*, 1978.

CHARLIE WATTS

Charles Robert Watts was born on June 2, 1941, at University College Hospital, London, to Charles and Lilian (*née* Eaves) Watts. Charlie and his sister Linda were raised in Islington and then later in Kingsbury, a fairly affluent North London suburb.

Considered one of the great rock drummers, Charlie has mostly eschewed the rock'n'roll lifestyle and to this day still retains the bemused mien of a jazzer who almost by chance fell in with 'the greatest rock'n'roll band in the world'.

Legend has it that a young Charlie was given a banjo by his parents but, bemused by the complicated chord book that came with the instrument, he took the banjo apart and, ingeniously using some glue and part of a Meccano kit, turned it into a drum. His parents, having got the message, took the brave decision to purchase their son a drum kit shortly after.

From his earliest days, jazz was always Charlie's first love. He's quoted as saying, "I wanted to be Charlie Parker", and he would listen to the likes of Thelonious Monk, Dizzy Gillespie and Lester Young over and over.

As a young man Charlie trained as a graphic designer and later one of his cartoons would grace the back of the sleeve for *Between The Buttons*. In 1964 he even published an illustrated children's book about Charlie Parker entitled *Ode To A High Flying Bird*.

His early musical career took him through stints in a number of skiffle and trad jazz bands to, eventually, a stint with Alexis Korner's Blues Incorporated. Eventually, however, and although he had several other intermittent and better-paid gigs, when the Stones came calling in January 1963 he consented to join up. With typical self-effacement, he said of his departure from Alexis' band, "I wasn't really good enough. They were such fantastic musicians; I couldn't keep up the pace. When I left Ginger Baker took over." His first gig with the band was at the Ealing Jazz Club on January 12, 1963.

Immediately the rhythm section bonded, not just personally but, more importantly, as musicians. They would form the bedrock of The Rolling Stones' sound for nigh on 30 years. It helped that both Bill and Charlie were considered the 'odd ones out'. Along with Ian Stewart, they were the sensible, stoical ones who offset the more flamboyant and outrageous behaviour of Mick, Brian, Keith and later, Andrew Loog Oldham.

Right: A well respected man, the ever dapper Mr Charlie Watts.

Being married at an early age certainly helped Charlie to take almost an outsider's perspective of the mania that would engulf the Stones. He had met his future wife Shirley some time before the band became successful; their only daughter, Seraphina, was born on March 18, 1968. It is testimony to the pair's enduring love for each other that they are still together more than 46 years later.

Although he was never tempted by many of the excesses that plagued the band, he did rather incongruously waver during the early part of the Eighties, when he started using heroin. Perversely, he says he was tempted to try the drug precisely because it was the last thing anyone would have expected him to do. It says a lot about the man that he managed to wean himself off the drug without recourse to expensive therapy and without public knowledge. Indeed, the whole episode would have remained private had Charlie not decided to reveal his secret some 30 years on.

It was during this period that, allegedly, a notorious altercation took place between the drummer and the singer in the band. With the Stones in disarray and the future looking bleak, the various members assembled in Amsterdam to try to resolve their differences. As the story goes, a rather refreshed Mick Jagger called Charlie's hotel room in the small hours and said to him, "Is that my drummer? Why don't you get your arse down here?" With this, Charlie promptly showered and shaved, donned a suit, went to Mick's room and said, "You're my fucking singer", before knocking Mick cold with a perfectly executed left-hook. Charlie, needless to say, is reticent when pursued on the subject.

Outside of the Stones, Charlie has continued to pursue his love of jazz. During the periods when the band has been dormant he has gigged and recorded with his own pick-up band and jazz orchestral; Charlie's big band which toured in the Eighties included such luminaries as Courtney Pine and Evan Parker. Later the Charlie Watts Quintet would feature singer Bernard Fowler who would go on to tour with the Stones throughout the Nineties and 'Noughties'. He also joined Ian Stewart for the Rocket 88 project, which released an eponymous album on Atlantic in 1981.

In June 1994, Charlie was diagnosed with throat cancer but after a course of extensive radiotherapy the cancer went into remission and he is now in rude health.

Keith Richards once said of his friend and occasional adversary Mick Jagger, 'Mick's rock, I'm roll': but really it's Charlie who is the rock AND the roll, for arguably without Charlie holding everyone together and being the go-between for the warring factions, the band could have split acrimoniously in the mid-Eighties. Being on equally friendly terms with both Mick and Keith, he is the voice of reason in the band and happily plays the role of diplomat when matters threaten to get out of hand, and it goes without saying that without his unfussy playing and solid backbeat, the Stones wouldn't be the band we know and love today, after over 50 years of making records together.

Left: Mr and Mrs Watts. They married in 1964.

Right: The ever dependable Charlie Watts, doing what he does best, May 2009.

INTO THE EIGHTIES

It took almost 19 months for Keith's bust in Toronto to come to trial. Eventually, in October 1978, and due to a combination of Keith's willingness to receive treatment for his addiction and the intervention of a young blind fan, who told the presiding judge that Keith had looked after her welfare when she had followed the band on tour, Keith was fined and let off, on condition he played a free benefit show in Toronto.

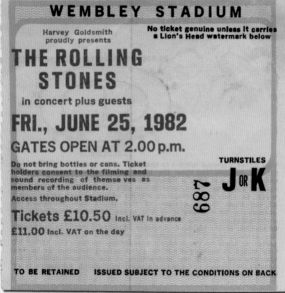

Left: June 1980, New York City – launch party for *Emotional Rescue*.

Above: Wembley Stadium ticket, London, June 1982.

Thus in April 1979 Keith and Ronnie's new band, The New Barbarians, which also included in its line-up Stanley Clark (bass), The Meters' Joseph Modelliste (drums), Ian McLagen (keyboards) and Bobby Keys on sax, played two shows along with The Rolling Stones at the Oshawa Civic Auditorium in Toronto. It would be the band's last live appearance for nigh on two-and-half-years.

With Keith and Ronnie heavily involved with The New Barbarians, and with Mick in the process of divorcing Bianca, the prospects for the Stones as they entered the new decade did not look particularly rosy. The traumas of Toronto had a put a dreadful strain on Mick and Keith's relationship, so it was with a certain amount of trepidation that the band got back together in June 1979 to begin work on what was to become *Emotional Rescue*. Work continued sporadically until mid-October, during which time Keith and Ronnie took time off for The New Barbarians to play at Knebworth with Led Zeppelin.

JUNE 20, 1980
Emotional Rescue (Rolling Stones COC 16015)

Dance (Part1)/Summer Romance/Send It To Me/Let Me Go/ Indian Girl/Where The Boys Go/Down In The Hole/Emotional Rescue/She's So Cold/All About You

Sadly, the creative and commercial high of *Some Girls* was not to be repeated. With everything that had been going down in the previous two years, though, it was hardly surprising. Tensions within the camp, and particularly between the Glimmer Twins, were running high. Creatively, Mick and Keith were after different sounds; Mick was all for moving forward and embracing the new sounds and technology of a new decade while Keith, perhaps inevitably, wanted the band to be more rootsy. Bill Wyman summed it up neatly: "Keith – guitars; Mick – dance." And, according to Keith, Mick wanted to have hits, while he himself 'couldn't give a f**k'. Apart from the track selection, mixing the album caused the most grief and almost took longer than the actual recording process. There were several altercations between Mick and Keith during this period. The rift, now a crack, was widening.

Although not as strong as its predecessor, the album still has the same pleasing eclectic hallmark, with songs ranging through several genres. 'Dance', co-written with Ronnie Wood, does what it says on the tin and was another clubland hit; 'Send It To Me' is another reggae-ish workout, with hilarious lyrics, and the stable of riff-tastic rockers includes 'Summer Romance', 'Where The Boys Go' and 'She's So Cold'. The closing track, 'All About You', is a wistful ballad, now something of a Keith trademark.

Surprisingly, the album was a massive number one hit in both the UK and the US, spending (for the Stones) a record seven weeks at the top of the Billboard Top 200.

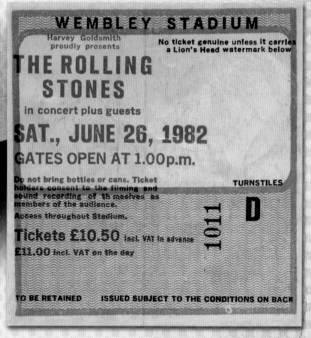

The lead-off single, 'Start Me Up' fired a shot across the bows of those critics who had claimed the band had gone soft. Originating as early as 1975, when it was conceived as a reggae jam during the sessions for *Black and Blue* it had somehow morphed into a bona-fide classic Stones rocker. The rest of the album is no slouch either. 'Waiting On A Friend' (another single) is an aching ballad, immortalized by a touching promo video. The killer track, though, is 'Slave', six minutes and 32 seconds of pure Stones raunchy sleaze powered by jazz giant Sonny Rollins' snaking sax solos.

Following its release the band embarked on a massive US tour that took in 50 shows in 28 cities, from the end of September to the middle of December. Once more the Stones had moved the goalposts when it came to tour production values. The stage and sets were spectacular, and at that time the largest ever built for a live performance. The striking artwork for the 224ft x 150ft set came from original paintings by Japanese artist Kazuhide Yamazaki. It was to be the last time the Stones would tour North America for eight long years.

AUGUST 28, 1981

Tattoo You (Rolling Stones Records CUNS 39114)

Start Me Up/Hang Fire/Slave/Little T&A/Black Limousine/ Neighbours/Worried About You/Tops/Heaven/No Use In Crying/ Waiting On A Friend

Unusually, the Stones chose not to tour *Emotional Rescue* and instead spent their time working on various other band and (in the case of Bill and Ronnie) solo projects. This also meant Mick and Keith could spend more time in the studio with engineer Chris Kimsey working on and cleaning up a number of songs that had been discarded from sessions going back (in some cases) as far as the beginning of the Seventies. What could have ended up as a rag-bag of out-takes instead emerged as an amazingly coherent body of work that stands proudly up against any of the band's latter-day catalogue.

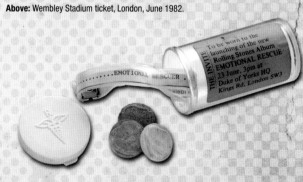

Left: Waiting to go on, Europe 1982. What is Mick wearing?

Above: The invitation to the *Emotional Rescue* launch party included hospital-related objects – even a wristband to wear.

Right: L.A. Coliseum, October 1981. Mick
has 100,000 fans eating out of his hands.

RONNIE WOOD

Born on June 1, 1947, in the West London suburb of Hillingdon, Ronald David Wood is the most junior member of the current line-up of The Rolling Stones. Along with his elder brothers Ted and Art, he was part of the first generation of his branch of the Wood clan to be born with the feel of solid *terra firma* under his boots; his father Arthur (Archie) and mother Mercy Leah (Lizzy) were both from families somewhat romantically known as water gypsies, and had been brought up on barges moored in the Paddington basin in central west London.

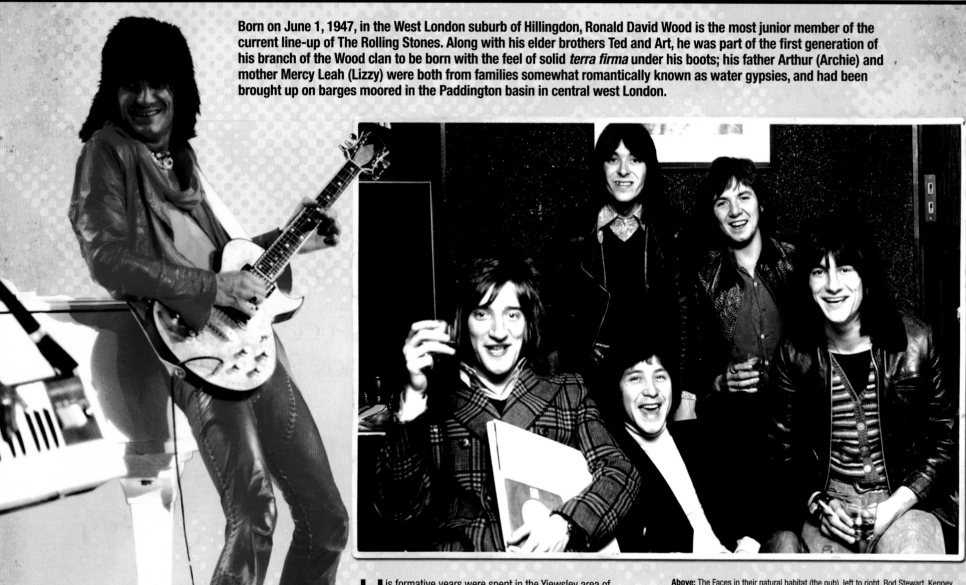

Above: The Faces in their natural habitat (the pub), left to right, Rod Stewart, Kenney Jones, Ian McLagen, Ronnie Lane, Ronnie Wood.

His formative years were spent in the Yiewsley area of Hillingdon, close to Heathrow Airport. He idolized his older brothers and when, as a callow teenager, Art picked up a guitar, Ronnie followed in his wake. Ronnie's first band, The Birds, formed with other local Yiewsley lads, successfully rode the Mod bandwagon and managed to attract a healthy local following which soon alerted a number of interested labels.

The Birds cut three singles for Decca but the chart eluded them, and once American West Coast icons and Dylan fetishists The Byrds had landed in the UK and usurped their name, the British Birds split, with Ronnie and bass player Kim Gardner joining The Creation. The Creation would become one of the great cult bands of the Sixties but Ronnie's stint in the band was short and he soon left to join the Jeff Beck Band which included his soon-to-be partner in crime, vocalist extraordinaire Rod Stewart. The band also featured long-time Stones associate Nicky Hopkins on piano.

solo album *I've Got My Own Album To Do*, but at this point The Faces were still a going concern and he wasn't about to leave them in the lurch. The Stones had recording sessions booked and a massive US tour to undertake and a number of other candidates were in the frame; indeed, both Harvey Mandel and Wayne Perkins were seriously considered for the role.

In the end it was Ronnie's easy-going personality and burgeoning relationship with both Mick and Keith that won the day, while his playing style perfectly complemented Keith's and harked back to the days when he and Brian Jones had almost interchangeable guitar parts. In the end a compromise was agreed and Ronnie was hired for the forthcoming US tour, and in December, when Rod announced that he was leaving The Faces, the deal was effectively sealed. However, Ronnie didn't become a bona fide, fully fledged and paid-up member of the Stones until the early Nineties, having been on a retainer, with

bonus payments for tours, up until that point. When, during the early years of his tenure, the Stones weren't working, Ronnie continued his solo work and various extra-curricular activities. His second solo album, *Now Look*, was released in 1975; featuring contributions from such luminaries as Bobby Womack, Willie Weeks, Mick Taylor and Andy Newmark, plus of course Keith, it's a mighty fine album of blues and R'n'B-infused boogie. Ronnie's third solo album, *Gimme Some Neck*, was released in 1979 and again Keith features strongly. He's aided and abetted by a whole host of current and former bandmates, including Mr Watts, Mr Jagger and Ian McLagen. Bobby Keys and Mick Fleetwood also join the party.

Keith and Ronnie would combine again in the New Barbarians, who would make their live debut as part of Keith's penance after the infamous Toronto bust in 1979. Later that year the band toured the US and supported Led Zeppelin (in what was to be their last live appearance) at Knebworth.

Incredibly, Ronnie has now been a part of The Rolling Stones for 35 years, exceeding Bill Wyman's time with the band. These days, when the band isn't working he fills his time playing the odd gig, releasing the occasional album and pursuing his love of art with his highly individual and successful portraits of his friends and fellow musicians.

Having cut two albums, *Truth* and *Beck-Ola*, with Beck and despite achieving a modicum of success in both the UK and the US, Ronnie and Rod departed to throw their lot in with Ronnie Lane, Ian McLagan and Kenney Jones, who along with Steve Marriott had enjoyed a roller-coaster ride as one of the key Mod bands of the era, The Small Faces. Marriott had left the band abruptly, disillusioned with both the artistic direction his bandmates wanted to take and with the band's management.

Now simply The Faces, their boozy image, amiable camaraderie and incendiary live performances soon garnered them a formidable reputation and this, along with Rod Stewart's successful parallel solo career (most of the band contributed to his solo albums), guaranteed them massive success on both sides of the Atlantic. Despite all this, Rod's solo work was soon overshadowing that of The Faces, and when soon after the release of the band's fourth long-player *Ooh La La* in 1974 he declared a dislike for the album, the band began to splinter. Mainstay and songwriter Ronnie Lane departed to pursue his own interests, and following a fraught US tour and a final single release Rod made the others' minds up for them and quit.

When Mick Taylor announced his departure from The Rolling Stones that year, it left the band in a massive quandary. On the face of it Ronnie was the ideal replacement, but in reality the issue was never that simple. Both Mick and Keith had contributed to Ronnie's

Above: A Ronnie trademark – his Telecaster, artworked for the Urban Jungle tour of 1989–90.

Right: Another of Ron's classic artworks, this one celebrating the *Forty Licks* tour.

UNDERCOVER AND ONWARDS

The mammoth North American tour that followed the release of *Tattoo You* was a huge earner for the Stones, but the length of the tour had only contrived to inflame relationships within the band again. Mick was now getting a serious business head on and was keen on maximizing revenue by filming a number of dates for a possible future cinematic and video release. A two-month tour of Europe in the summer of 1982 was in the planning stages but initially looked as if it wouldn't be financially viable. Mick, perhaps inevitably, wasn't going to schlep around Europe if the tour was only going to break even; the rest of the band were keen to get on with it. With a little bit of tweaking, it was then estimated that each band member would clear in excess of $500,000: not bad for approximately 70 hours of hard toil on stage!

Arguments broke out again over the need for extensive rehearsals for the tour. Mick, ever the perfectionist, wanted the band to commit to five weeks, whereas Keith thought they only needed one.

The tour eventually kicked off on May 26 at the Capital Theatre in Aberdeen, Scotland, followed by two more theatre shows before a return to the band's roots with a 'secret' show at the 300-capacity 100 Club in London, where the band were billed as Diz and the Doormen. Club shows would become a fixture of the band's London sojourns on subsequent tours, usually accompanied by a media feeding frenzy and a mad scramble for tickets.

Then, utilizing almost exactly the same stage set as they had in North America the previous year, the band set off playing outdoor stadiums throughout Europe. The tour took them through the Netherlands, West Germany, France, Sweden, Italy, Austria, Spain, Switzerland and Ireland, culminating with a show at Roundhay Park in Leeds on July 25.

June 1 saw the release of the Stones' third live album. Entitled *Still Life (American Concert 1981)*, it documented the previous year's tour and, aside from the standard edition, was released as a limited-edition picture disc. Some early pressings wrongly contained alternative tracks; these discs now fetch a small fortune on the collectors' market. Though not an essential Stones live recording, the band's strong popularity ensured that the album was a top 5 hit in the UK and US.

After a summer break, the band met up in Paris in November with financial advisor Prince Rupert Lowenstein to discuss plans for the future. These included a new studio album for the summer of 1983 and a compilation album that would necessitate a deal with Allen Klein to utilize some of the band's Sixties repertoire.

Tattoo You had been a rescue job, albeit an incredibly good one; hugely successful, it had utilized and cleaned up almost a decade's-worth of odds and sods to great effect. However, conscious of the fact they desperately needed to record some new material, the Stones, now close to the 20th anniversary of their first single release, assembled at the Pathé Marconi Studios in Paris to commence work. They were joined by engineer Chris Kimsey, there to oversee the Glimmer Twins' production methods.

Below: Back to their roots, live at the 100 Club in London, May 31, 1982.

Opposite: Older and wiser, sort of. The Rolling Stones, suited and booted, 1981

Again, there were clashes over the direction the band should take musically. Mick was all for embracing new studio techniques, whereas Keith wanted to keep it simple. He recalls coining the none-too-flattering nickname 'Brenda' for Mick around this time. It seemed Mick was trying to control the band and Keith in particular resented this. He attempted to get around the situation by arranging to be at the studio at times when he knew that Mick would not. Hence, on a typical day, Mick would work from midday to around 5pm, while Keith would keep more nocturnal hours, working from midnight until five in the morning. Keith has been damning in his criticism of Mick while Mick, diplomatically, has kept quiet. It is tempting to think that if Mick had not exercised a modicum of control, the Stones would have been a spent force.

NOVEMBER 7:
Undercover (Rolling Stones Records 1654361)

Undercover Of The Night/She Was Hot/Tie You Up (The Pain Of Love)/Wanna Hold You/Feel On Baby/Too Much Blood/Pretty Beat Up/Too Tough/All The Way Down/It Must Be Hell

Sessions for *Undercover* were eventually completed at the Hit Factory in New York, with the legendary Jamaican rhythm section of Sly Dunbar and Robbie Shakespeare on board. Ex-Allman Brother Chuck Leavell was also present, contributing keyboards; Chuck would later be a permanent fixture as part of the Stones' extended touring band.

The title track of the album was released a week before as a single and was accompanied by a promo video that caused a storm of controversy. Banned by the BBC, the video was eventually premiered in its entirety on a special late-night slot on London Weekend Television and showed a kidnapper (played by Keith) shooting a journalist (Mick) at close range. Director Julien Temple, who had previously worked with the Sex Pistols, was forced to go on TV to defend it. It proved that the Stones, now into their forties, could still kick up a storm when needed.

Undercover is a child born of the Eighties. It's by no means a classic, but has stood the test of time remarkably well. For that we have to thank Mick's magpie instincts, for it's the tracks which show his innovative tendencies which work best, particularly the title track, 'Too Much Blood' with its African rhythms and the sado-masochistic ' Tie You Up (The Pain of Love)'.

DIRTY WORK,
BUT SOMEBODY HAS TO DO IT ...

Prior to the release of *Undercover*, **the Stones inked yet another lucrative record deal. This time it was a worldwide deal with CBS and was expected to net the band in excess of £28 million for four albums' worth of material. CBS would have to wait nearly three years for the band's next new studio album. Internecine warfare was splitting the Stones asunder and to many it seemed entirely possible that the Stones could cease to be a going concern in the not too distant future. The bad feeling between Mick and Keith was exacerbated when it emerged that while negotiating the band's deal with Walter Yetnikoff at CBS, Mick had in fact put his name to a multi-million-dollar solo contract.**

Left: Mick and Tina Turner playing Live Aid, JFK Stadium Philadelphia, July 13, 1985.

With Mick otherwise engaged, the rest of the band turned to other pursuits. Keith, having wed his new flame Patti Hansen on his 40th birthday the previous December, was enjoying married life. Bill, meanwhile, having busied himself compiling and filming links for *Rewind*, a video companion to a new hits compilation (released on July 24, 1984) was embarking on his infamous liaison with the teenage Mandy Smith. Charlie at this point seemed to be on a permanent bender, although the sordid details would not emerge until a good 20 years after the event.

Mick commenced work on his solo project in May, recording at Compass Point Studios in Nassau in the Bahamas with a host of prominent musicians including the Chic duo of Bernard Edwards and Nile Rodgers, Jeff Beck, Pete Townshend, Sly and Robbie and Herbie Hancock. After a fractious band meeting in New York in October (Bill was absent) it was agreed that they should get together in Paris early in the New Year to start recording a new album.

Much to the rest of the band's chagrin, the album sessions were delayed when Mick's own recording schedule overran: and when he did turn up, he was in no position to contribute his usual clutch of new songs, as most of them had been used up on his solo album. This obviously infuriated Keith. Charlie, who was going through his own personal crisis at this time, cut his hand badly and, unable to drum, flew back to England for a period of recuperation.

With the initial sessions not gelling the band hired an outside producer, the highly influential and cutting-edge Steve Lilywhite, the first time they had done such a thing since using Jimmy Miller on *Goats Head Soup* in 1973. Lilywhite, although dismayed by the fractious atmosphere, did by all accounts help to smooth things over and offer an impartial ear.

Towards the end of May, meetings were held to discuss the possibility of the band playing the forthcoming worldwide Live Aid show. Bob Geldof even flew to Paris to persuade the band to do it

but there was a marked reluctance to disrupt the recording process. At the last minute, however, Mick decided he wanted to be involved and cut the single 'Dancing In The Street' with David Bowie. On the day itself Mick performed with Tina Turner while Keith, along with Ronnie and Bob Dylan, played an embarrassingly ramshackle acoustic set.

On December 12 the band were united in grief when Ian Stewart died of a heart attack in a doctor's waiting room in Harley Street; he was 47. The following February the band were on stage together for the first time in nearly four years when they played a tribute show for Stu at the 100 Club in London's Oxford Street. They were joined on stage by Simon Kirke (ex-Free), Jeff Beck, Eric Clapton, Jack Bruce and Pete Townshend.

Below: Ronnie, Bob Dylan and Keith during their somewhat ramshackle Live Aid performance.

MARCH 24, 1986

Dirty Work (Rolling Stones Records CBS 86321)

One Hit (To The Body)/Fight/Harlem Shuffle/Hold Back/Too Rude/Winning Ugly/Back To Zero/Dirty Work/Had It With You/Sleep Tonight

The miserable-looking cover shot of the band (taken by Annie Liebovitz) probably says it all about *Dirty Work*. The Stones album least loved by protagonists, critics and fans alike is a tough body of work to plough through. It says it all that the lead-off single was the rather perfunctory cover of 'Harlem Shuffle', the first cover version the Stones had chosen for a single (apart from live tracks) since 'Little Red Rooster' in 1964.

'One Hit (To The Body)', chosen as a follow-up single, is worthy enough, all clattering drums and vicious guitar work. The video, appropriately, had Mick and Keith swinging punches at each other. Elsewhere, the dubby reggae of 'Too Rude' (sung by Keith) is possibly one of the band's better ventures into that particular genre and 'Sleep Tonight' is one of Keith's best latter-day ballads. On a sombre note, the album is dedicated to Ian Stewart with the legend, "Thanks, Stu, for 25 years of boogie-woogie", and closes with 33 seconds of Stu playing Big Bill Broonzy's 'Key To The Highway'.

Unsurprisingly, the band chose not to go on the road to promote *Dirty Work*. If Keith was aggrieved, then the rest of the band were relieved. Even the usually taciturn Bill Wyman was moved to admit that it could have spelt the end had the band been forced to spend long months on the road together.

Soon Mick would be otherwise engaged in the follow-up to his debut album and a frustrated Keith would finally start on his own solo project. In the downtime Charlie resurrected his love for jazz and toured America and the UK with his orchestra. A live album, *Live At Fulham Town Hall*, was released in February 1987.

Making up instead of breaking up

Mick's second solo outing, *Primitive Cool*, appeared on September 14, 1987. Keith, having signed his own solo deal, with Virgin, released his debut, *Talk Is Cheap* just over a year later, on October 3, 1988. Both were relatively well received and achieved respectable sales and chart placings.

With the band in limbo and the two main players at loggerheads, the press had a field day. This wasn't helped by a number of interviews Mick and Keith gave at the time. Mick had complained to a *Daily Mirror* journalist that "Keith wanted to run the band single-handedly" and that "I don't really feel that we can work together any more." In *The Sun*, Keith countered with, "He should stop being like Peter Pan and grow up", adding: "He has told me to my face that he cannot work with me, but he cannot say why." Even Bill, when asked by MTV if the Stones were finished, said, "It looks that way."

Without hearing Mick Jagger's side of the story, we only have Keith Richards' version to explain why, in January 1989, there was a sudden thaw in their relationship. Keith, being Keith, has stated that it was Mick who made the call, and that "Mick needed the Stones more that the Stones needed Mick." The pair met in Barbados to iron out their differences and within a couple of weeks were attending the band's induction into the Rock'n'Roll Hall Of Fame at an awards ceremony in New York, accompanied by their erstwhile guitarist Mick Taylor and the present incumbent, Ronnie Wood.

By the middle of March the band were rehearsing new material at Eddy Grant's Blue Wave studio in Barbados before decamping to George Martin's Air studios in Montserrat to commence recording. They also began formulating plans to tour North America later that year. Despite not having played together for nearly four years, the sessions proved remarkably productive. With producer Chris Kimsey back on board to aid the Glimmer Twins, the band worked up more than 20 new songs.

Below: Mick goes solo. Recording *Primitive Cool*, Wisseloord Studios, Hilversum, Holland, December 1986.

Bottom Left: Together again for *Dirty Work*, but not looking entirely happy about it.

67

1989: *STEEL WHEELS*

AUGUST 29:

Steel Wheels (CBS 465752)

Sad Sad Sad/Mixed Emotions/Terrifying/Hold On To Your Hat/Hearts For Sale/Blinded By Love/Rock And A Hard Place/Can't Be Seen/Almost Hear You Sigh/Continental Drift/Break The Spell/Slipping Away

Although almost universally praised on its release, it's unlikely *Steel Wheels* will ever find its way on to any of those ubiquitous lists of the greatest rock'n'roll albums of all time. Indeed, it would struggle to register among the top albums released in 1989: but after the travails of the previous five years or so, it is a pleasing return to form – of sorts.

Recorded in relatively little time (for the Stones), there's a real sense of purpose about the album as a whole, and it has a flow and a direction that certainly wasn't apparent on their previous two offerings.

The first single, 'Mixed Emotions', perhaps alluded to the protagonists' state of mind regarding the sudden about-turn that enabled Mick and Keith to come together again. It was an odd choice for a single; 'Rock And A Hard Place', which is of a similar ilk, is a far better song but was relegated to the status of a follow-up release. But it's where the band go off-piste that the album gets interesting. 'Continental Drift' features the master musicians of Joujouka in Northern Morocco; Mick had, out of the blue, received a letter from one of their number, Bachir Attar, who had only been a small child when Brian Jones had recorded them back in 1969. Mick, Keith and Ronnie duly jetted off to Tangiers towards the end of the recording process and managed to create an otherworldly soundscape featuring the Sufis' massed drumming and pan pipes.

Elsewhere, 'Break The Spell', has a sparse, lolloping, rockabilly sound that suggests the band had been listening to The Stray Cats; indeed, the New York trio had supported the Stones on a number of dates on their last US tour. 'Slipping Away' was a warm, affecting Keith ballad of the kind which would become his trademark over the next few albums and 'Almost Hear You Sigh', another single, is a classy mid-tempo ballad co-written with Steve Jordan, who had worked on Keith's solo album.

Steel Wheels fared well, hitting number 3 in the Billboard 200 and going on to sell more than two million copies in the US alone. It reached number 2 in the UK album chart.

Right: Bill grins and bears it, Steel Wheels tour, Atlanta, Georgia, November 24, 1989.

Out on the road

The mammoth North American tour, which kicked off at the end of August at Veterans' Stadium in Philadelphia and concluded on December 20 with three dates at the Convention Center in Atlantic City, was a landmark in more ways than one. It was the first run by Canadian promoter Michael Cohl. Having negotiated a deal with the Stones in the early months of 1989, he literally took ownership of the tour – setting up sponsorship (including a $3.5 million deal with Budweiser) and merchandizing deals and sorting out television, radio and film rights.

It was the first of a number of megadeals that would see the Stones rinse the corporate dollar over the next 20 years.

The Stones played to more than three million people in the US and Canada that autumn and winter. They then headed off for their first live dates in Japan the following February, where they would gross around £20 million from just ten shows.

The tour would be recalibrated and presented as the *Urban Jungle* tour when it hit Europe in May the following year. The tour came to a close on a balmy night at Wembley Stadium on August 25, 1991. It was to be Bill Wyman's final show as a member of The Rolling Stones.

Left: The now traditional curtain call, Atlanta, Georgia, November 24, 1989.

BILL WYMAN

The oldest member of the original quintet, Bill Wyman was born William George Perks in Lewisham Hospital in South-East London on October 23, 1936. He officially changed his name by deed poll to Wyman (after a friend he'd met during his National Service, Lee Whyman) in 1964. Bill was the eldest of six children, all born to William George Perks senior and his wife Kathleen May. His father, a bricklayer by trade, taught himself piano and accordion and was much in demand at local social events.

A bright child, Bill's education was curtailed at an early age when, with his father unemployed, he was forced to leave school and get a job to help support his family. Although interested in music from an early age (he had piano lessons around the age of 10) it wasn't until 1954, at the age of 18, when he joined the RAF to do his National Service that he bought his first guitar and started to learn to play. Unlike the rest of The Rolling Stones, though, it was the rock 'n roll of Elvis, Bill Haley and Jerry Lee Lewis that attracted Bill rather than the blues and R'n'B of Muddy Waters and John Lee Hooker. It wasn't long before Bill, along with a few like-minded souls, had formed a skiffle group.

Completing National Service in January 1958, Bill was soon back into the swing of civilian life, attending rock'n'roll, skiffle and jazz concerts around London. He also had a penchant for dancing and it was through this particular hobby that he would meet his first wife, Diane. After a short courtship they were married in October 1959. The following year Bill made his first inroads into the world of popular music. Inspired by a work colleague, Steve Carroll, who played in an amateur band, Bill splashed out the not inconsiderable sum of £52 for his first electric guitar, a Burns.

With the band, now named The Cliftons, gaining in proficiency, Bill had something of an epiphany when he attended a Barron Knights gig in August 1961. They had something that the Cliftons were missing – a bass player. Struck by the power of the instrument and the way it anchored the Barron Knights' sound, Bill immediately decided to switch from the guitar.

By the end of 1962, the Cliftons had built a solid reputation as a no-nonsense rock'n'roll outfit and were gigging regularly around London, Kent and Essex. Their path would cross that of the nascent Rollin' Stones when, unknown to the rest of The Cliftons, drummer Tony Chapman answered an ad in *Melody Maker* posted by the Stones. It was Chapman, who after Dick Taylor had left the Stones, helped Bill get the gig that would change his life for ever.

Legend has it that Mick, Brian and Keith were particularly aloof when they first met Bill, but all this changed at their first rehearsal together when Bill unloaded his equipment from his car. A brand-new Vox AC30 amp and a massive speaker cabinet Bill had built himself completely dwarfed the Stones' gear and, after another tentative rehearsal, Bill was in. His first gig with the Stones was on December 14, 1962, at the Ricky Tick Club at the Star and Garter Hotel in Windsor.

Above: Bill gets his picture taken by his son Stephen at village fete, Lee Chapel South, Baslidon, Essex. May 29, 1967.

Right: Vintage Bill, European tour, 1973.

Bill's contribution to The Rolling Stones' sound and to some of their greatest songs is often overlooked. Because he didn't receive any writing credits, it's often assumed that all he did was just lay down the bassline. Nothing could be further from the truth; he was a vital cog in the composition of a number of Stones classics, including, 'Paint It Black', and 'Jumping Jack Flash', and added the distinctive bowed double bass to 'Ruby Tuesday'. 'In Another Land', from *Their Satanic Majesties*, ostensibly a Wyman solo effort, was released as a single in the US. Another Wyman composition, 'Downtown Suzie', recorded during the *Beggars Banquet* sessions, finally saw the light of day on the *Metamorphosis* compilation in 1975.

Less well documented are Bill's forays into production and his work with other acts. From early as the mid-Sixties Bill was involved with such diverse acts as young British rock band The End, whom he managed up until the end of the Sixties, R'n'B singer Bobbie Miller and British blues-rock band The Groundhogs. When The End mutated into Tucky Buzzard (who were signed for a time to Deep Purple's eponymous Purple label), Bill produced a number of their albums through the early Seventies.

Frustrated by the lack of opportunities to contribute

Above: Still Rolling. Live with the Rhythm Kings.

his own songs to the Stones canon, Bill embarked on a successful solo career in the mid-Seventies. Two albums, *Monkey Grip* (1974) and *Stone Alone* (1976), each garnered favourable reviews and a modicum of success, but it wasn't until the release of the single '(Si Si) Je Suis Un Rock Star' in 1981 that he had an international hit.

After the mammoth *Steel Wheels* and *Urban Jungle* tours of 1989–90, Bill announced to the other band members that he was leaving the fold. By his own admission he hadn't particularly enjoyed the rigours of the road for some time, and with no new Stones activity planned for the immediate future, he felt it was an opportune moment to jump ship. Naturally, the others tried to persuade him to change his mind and it wasn't until January 1993 that a formal announcement was made regarding his departure.

Now happily married to Suzanne Accosta and with three young daughters, Bill continues to play live and pursues his hobbies of photography and archaeology.

1991—93: KEEP ON ROLLIN'

January 1991 found the Stones in the studio again. Several hours' worth of material from the *Steel Wheels/Urban Jungle* tours was being mixed and collated for a proposed live album that would be the last of their current deal with CBS. As part of the process two new songs were recorded at the Hit Factory in London and these would be Bill Wyman's last recordings with the group.

In a move that pre-empted the now common marketing ploy of adding new or unreleased songs to greatest hits packages and live albums, 'Highwire' and 'Sex Drive' were tagged on to the *Flashpoint* live album released at the beginning of April 1981. In another marketing-led move in the US, a special limited-edition two-CD version of *Flashpoint* was released. The second disc was entitled *Collectibles* and featured ten 'rare' and previously unreleased tracks including a near-seven-minute-long version of 'Rock And A Hard Place', and the eight-and-a-half-minute version of 'Miss You'.

'Highwire', written about the futility of the (first) Gulf War, was released as a single to promote *Flashpoint* and when the promo video was shown *Top Of The Pops*, the BBC censored the song by editing out the first verse. The funky 'Sex Drive' was also released as a single later in the year accompanied by an appropriately salacious video.

In October 1991, the *Live At The Max* concert film was released. Filmed in the huge IMAX format and shot over several dates on the European leg of the *Urban Jungle* tour, the film was a spectacular document of The Rolling Stones live experience.

In November, the band signed another multi-million-pound record deal, this time with Richard Branson's Virgin Records. In addition to the rights to release the band's forthcoming studio projects, it also gave Virgin control over the Stones' post-Klein catalogue from *Sticky Fingers* onwards.

Aside from group activity, the individual band members now had time to pursue their own solo careers and other assorted projects. Keith, who was already contracted to Virgin as a solo artist, began recording his second album, *Main Offender*, in New York while Mick, recruiting producer Rick Rubin, settled in LA to begin work on what was to become his third solo outing, *Wandering Spirit*. Charlie, meanwhile, was busy with his jazz quintet and would release three

albums in the five-year gap between Stones studio records. Ronnie was also active, recording his fifth solo album, *Slide On This*, with a stellar line-up of sidemen including Joe Elliot, The Edge, Simon Kirke, Ian McLagan and Charlie Watts.

April 1993 saw the band tentatively reconvene in Barbados to begin preparations for their next studio album: but there was the problem of replacing Bill Wyman. Rather than auditioning while recording, as they had done before ultimately recruiting Ronnie Wood during the *Black and Blue* sessions, the band set up auditions at New York's S.I.R Studios in June 1993. Having rehearsed with a number of high-profile session players, including Joey Spampinato (who had played with Keith at a special Chuck Berry tribute concert back in 1986), Garry Tallent (from Bruce Springsteen's E Street Band) and Larry Taylor (who had played with Canned Heat and John Mayall), they eventually settled on Daryll Jones.

Jones was a precocious talent who had played in Miles Davis' band at the tender age of 18 and also featured on Sting's multi-million-selling *Dream Of The Blue Turtles* album as well as also playing with the likes of Herbie Hancock, Madonna, Cher, Peter Gabriel and Eric Clapton. He would not become a fully-fledged member of The Rolling Stones but, like Chuck Leavell (keyboards), Bernard Fowler (vocals), Lisa Fischer (vocals) and Blondie Chaplin (guitar and vocals), he would be a hired hand and a permanent fixture on Stones tours and recordings over the next few years.

July 26, 1993, saw Mick Jagger celebrate his 50th birthday. Having over the years ridiculed the idea of rock'n'roll bands playing on into middle age, Mick was now playing out the role himself.

Top: Keith launching *Main Offender* with the X-Pensive Winos.

Above: Keith rehearsing with Steve Cropper, Robert Cray and Bob Dylan.

Left: With their new paymaster, Virgin Records' boss Richard Branson.

With Daryll Jones on board, and with new producer Don Was at the controls, recording started again in earnest in Ireland, first at Ronnie's home studio in Kildare and then at Windmill Studios in Dublin. At Ronnie's house, Keith had a run-in with a rock'n'roll legend – Jerry Lee Lewis. He was staying close by so the band, being fans, invited him over to play. A long, boozy jam ensued, with Jerry Lee apparently assuming the session was being recorded. Not happy with what he was hearing, he started to belittle the band, much to Keith's annoyance, and Keith allegedly offered to take Jerry Lee outside to 'sort out their differences'. Thankfully common sense prevailed.

On November 22, 1993, the band's first release on Virgin hit the stores. Entitled *Jump Back*, it was an 18-track single CD (double vinyl) compilation of the best of the post-Klein catalogue. It quickly went gold in the UK and across Europe but, strangely, wasn't released in the UK until 2004.

As part of the deal with Virgin, all the albums from *Brown Sugar* through to *Tattoo You* were re-mastered by Bob Ludwig and re-issued in a mini-vinyl CD format in 1994.

KEITH RICHARDS

An only child, Keith Richards was born on Saturday, December 18, 1943, in the Livingstone Hospital, Dartford, Kent. His father, Herbert William Richards, was of Welsh descent. His family had moved to Walthamstow, North-East London, in the late 1800s. His mother Doris, also born in Wales, was one of seven sisters. His parents had met while working in the same factory in Edmonton, North London. Keith's earliest memories reveal an introverted child who hated school but loved the outdoor life. Keith and his pals would spend idyllic hours getting up to mischief on Dartford Heath and in the surrounding neighbourhood.

It was Keith's maternal grandfather, the exotically named Theodore Augustus Dupree, who aroused Keith's love of music from an early age. Gus, as he was affectionately known, was a First World War veteran and had run a dance band in the 1930s. He was also something of a multi-instrumentalist, playing at various times the saxophone, violin and, latterly, the guitar. Indeed, it was Gus who first taught Keith some rudimentary chords on the guitar.

At the age of 11 Keith played what he refers to as the most prestigious gig of his life. As a member of the Dartford Tech school choir Keith, a soprano, sang for the young Queen Elizabeth II at Westminster Abbey. However, his stint as a star chorister was to be brief, for when his voice broke a year later he was out on his ear.

As music became an obsession, he would listen to Radio Luxembourg through the night, twisting the aerial around to aid the notoriously bad reception. Here he would discover Elvis and a number of the other early rock'n'roll greats – Eddie Cochran, Gene Vincent, Little Richard and Buddy Holly.

Expelled from school aged 15, he was given a lucky break when his art teacher, recognizing Keith's talent at drawing, managed to secure him a place at Sidcup Art College. By this time he had taken delivery of his first guitar, a Rosetti acoustic, bought for him by his mother.

Thrown in with a bunch of like-minded bohemians and ne'er-do-wells, Keith was in his element. Soon a group of friends were hanging out together comparing musical tastes and jamming. Then came that fateful day in December 1961 when Keith bumped into Mick Jagger on Dartford station. Immediately they became soul brothers. Keith recalls that they were inseparable, going to gigs, perusing record stores all over London, learning hundreds of songs and even holidaying together. Their early repertoire included Chuck Berry's 'Around And Around' and 'Reelin' And Rockin', Jimmy Reed's 'Bright Lights, Big City' and 'La Bamba', which had been a huge hit for Richie Valens in 1958.

Above: A 1957 Gibson Les Paul Custom guitar, customised by Keith.

Opposite: Keith gets made up for the 'She Was Hot' video shoot.

Realizing that music was his true calling, Keith quit Sidcup Art College in order to concentrate on putting a band together. He did make one half-hearted attempt to use his education to land a 'proper' job, when he attended an interview at advertising firm J Walter Thompson, but in truth this was more of a gesture to appease his teacher at college than a genuine effort to join the white-collar agency. Keith was always going to go through life on his terms.

Throughout the tempestuous first two decades of the Stones, Keith cultivated an air of rock'n'roll rebellion. There is no doubt that his relationship with Anita Pallenberg was a big factor in this. The Italian-born model and actress broadened his horizons significantly and coaxed Keith out of his shell. Their relationship was almost pre-ordained to be a doomed one, however, and once Keith had weaned himself off heroin it was always going to peter out.

Throughout the Stones' career, Keith has more often than not been the one seen as keenest to keep the band's integrity intact. Even though the band could arguably have split apart when Keith's drug problems took their toll in the mid-Seventies, and then again during the 'World War Three' disputes between him and Mick a decade later, one suspects Keith would move heaven and earth to keep the flame burning.

Unlike Mick, Keith has never really shown an interest in any other activity than making music. However, he has famously made a brief incursion into the world of acting with his hilarious portrayal of Captain Teague in the third *Pirates Of The Caribbean* film, *At World's End* (2007).

His relationship with American model Patti Hansen, whom he met in 1979, has settled Keith down and when not working he seems happy living in his own unique vision of idyllic domesticity in the house they built in Connecticut in 1991.

'The Human Riff', 'lawless guitar-slinger', 'the world's most elegantly wasted human being'; all these epithets have been used to describe the man who embodies not only the spirit of The Rolling Stones, but the very essence of rock'n'roll itself.

In recent years there has been a great deal of self-mythologising, not least within the 564 pages of Keith's autobiography *Life* (for which he was paid an advance of over $7 million), but there is no doubt Keith Richards is the inspiration for all those wannabe young rock'n'rollers with their rooster-like haircuts and skinny jeans, who populate the lower reaches of the charts to this day. He's been quoted as saying he'll only give up playing 'when I croak' and there's no reason to disbelieve him. Meanwhile, the man with the skin of a rhinoceros and the constitution of an ox just keeps on rollin'.

Above: Art Collins' Tour pass from the New Barbarians tour of 1979. Art was Executive VP in charge of The Rolling Stones in the US from 1980 to 1986.

Opposite: Keith and Patti Hansen attend the premier of the *Stones in Exile* documentary, New York, May 11, 2010.

Opposite inset: Keith as Captain Jack Sparrow's (Johnny Depp) father, Captain Teague in *At World's End*, the third *Pirates of The Caribbean* movie, in 2007.

Right: In rude health, launching his autobiography, *Life* in London, November 3, 2010. It quickly became a bestseller.

1994: VOODOO LOUNGE

JULY 11, 1994

Voodoo Lounge (Virgin V2750)

Love Is Strong/You Got Me Rocking/Sparks Will Fly/The Worst/
New Faces/Moon Is Up/Out Of Tears/I Go Wild/Brand New Car/
Sweethearts Together/Suck On The Jugular/Blinded By Rainbows/
Baby Break It Down/Thru and Thru/Mean Disposition/

Five years on from *Steel Wheels*, the Stones released their 20th
studio album. It had been 30 years since their debut. Hailed as a
return to form by many critics, it certainly did the business chart-
wise, hitting the number 1 slot in the UK and in France and peaking
at number 2 in the *Billboard* 200 in the US.

Although the rancour and mistrust that had lain heavily between
Mick and Keith had mostly dissipated by the time recording was
under way, there were still bones of contention between the pair
which needed to be chewed upon and spat out. Not least was the
musical direction the band should take as they entered their fourth
decade together. It was new producer Don Was who would act as
diplomat extraordinaire this time around.

Born in Detroit, Michigan, Was had made his name as part of
the hugely influential Was (Not Was), who had pioneered a hybrid
rock/dance/disco formula on the painfully hip ZE Records in the
early Eighties. They scored a number of massive worldwide hits,
including 'Walk The Dinosaur' and 'Spy In The House Of Love'.
Since then Was had become something of a musical chameleon
and had worked with acts as diverse as Bonnie Raitt, The B52s,
Neil Diamond, Roy Orbison, Elton John and Iggy Pop. He had a
great knack for bringing a
cutting-edge sonic feel to so-
called 'heritage' acts.

Although not Keith's choice,
Was soon ingratiated himself
with the guitarist with his
no-nonsense approach. As
it transpired, Keith ended
up being happier with the
finished article than Mick.
Mick had wanted the album
to sound more experimental
but the now thick-as-
thieves duo of Keith and
Don Was had vetoed this
idea and gone down a
more traditional route.

Although by no means
a landmark Rolling Stones
album, *Voodoo Lounge*

does have its moments, notably in the opening track (and first
single) 'Love Is Strong'. With its powerhouse drums, dual Keith and
Ronnie guitar attack and some sublime harmonica-playing from
Mick, it's a latter-day Stones gem, made even more memorable by
the promo video, directed by David Fincher, showing the Stones
as giants picking their way across the Manhattan skyline. Second
single 'You Got Me Rocking' is the bastard offspring of 'If You Can't
Rock Me' from the *It's Only Rock 'n' Roll* album and is a staple of
the band's live set to this day.

There's a batch of great ballads here too, including Keith's 'Thru
And Thru' and 'The Worst', and the album's third single, 'Out Of
Tears' on which keyboard player Chuck Leavell excels, while the
baroque prettiness of 'New Faces' proved they could still write pop
songs as well as anyone. It harks back to more innocent times and
wouldn't sound out of place on *Between The Buttons*. Meanwhile
the Latin-tinged 'Sweethearts Together' finds Mick and Keith
sharing harmonies on what could be construed as an ironic nod to
their often strained relationship.

As with more recent Stones albums, there is a sense of quantity
over quality. With CD now the dominant format, and featuring 15
songs, the album clocks in at more than 62 minutes, a good 20
minutes more than the average long-playing vinyl record. At least
three of the songs here wouldn't have been missed.

As if to prove the Stones were up to speed with emerging
trends and technology, a *Voodoo Lounge* CDROM was released
simultaneously with the album. Now something of a curio, it enabled
the fans to 'wander round the *Voodoo Lounge*, meet the Stones (and
others) in mysterious circumstances and to solve puzzles'.

Above: The band launch
Voodoo Lounge, Pier 60,
New York City, May 3,
1994.

On August 1, after six weeks of rehearsals in Toronto including a 'surprise' warm-up club gig at the RPM Club, the band kicked off the *Voodoo Lounge* tour at the RFK Stadium in Washington DC. The tour would end more than a year later, at the end of August 1995, and be truly worldwide, taking in shows in South America (Brazil, Argentina and Chile), South Africa, Japan, Australia and New Zealand. The European leg took in 39 shows including Budapest and Prague.

The most sought-after tickets were for the small 'theatre' shows at The Paradiso in Amsterdam, L'Olympia in Paris and the Brixton Academy in London, where the band performed a more stripped-down set of older and more acoustic songs.

NOVEMBER 14, 1995
Stripped (Virgin V 2801)
Street Fighting Man/Like A Rolling Stone/Not Fade Away/Shine A Light/The Spider And The Fly/I'm Free/Wild Horses/Let It Bleed/Dead Flowers/Slipping Away/Angie/Love In Vain/Sweet Virginia/Little Baby

Stripped is The Rolling Stones' take on the *MTV* 'Unplugged' live acoustic album format that had proved massively successful in the late Eighties and early Nineties for acts as diverse as Mariah Carey, Nirvana and Paul McCartney, among a host of others. *Stripped*, however, is not fully live nor fully acoustic, but an amalgam of live performance (taken from the Paradiso, L'Olympia and Brixton shows of the *Voodoo Lounge* tour) and rehearsals recorded earlier in the year in Japan. The cover of Bob Dylan's 'Like A Rolling Stone' was released as a single and the album was a top 10 hit in both the US and the UK.

Right: Entourage AAA pass, Voodoo Lounge tour, 1994-95.

Below: Live in Germany on the European leg of the Voodoo Lounge tour, 1995.

Left: Mick, or "Brenda" as Keith calls him, flies the flag for good old Blighty, New York, 1994.

Opposite: One half of the Glimmer Twins, Keith on his knees, New York City, 1994.

1997: BRIDGES TO BABYLON

After the frenetic activity of the previous couple of years, there was a hiatus of sorts in 1996. Keen to make a more modern record than he thought the Stones were capable of, Mick was contemplating another solo venture, this time with renowned dance producers The Dust Brothers on board. Indeed, he went as far as recording demos in Atlanta, Georgia.

Keith, meanwhile, was reassembling his occasional band The X-pensive Winos in Jamaica while Charlie was busy recording his third Quintet album in London. It wasn't until early October that the idea of any new Stones activity was mooted, when Mick, Keith and Ronnie met up in New York to discuss plans. Whilst Keith and Ronnie were eager to start a new Stones project, Mick was less than keen, feeling once more that the band format was stifling his creativity. However, a compromise was reached whereby they would try out a number of different producers and, if necessary, work independently of each other. They would retain Don Was as an executive producer to help pull the project together. While making plans for new material, the Stones also served up a treat from the past; on October 14 – a mere 18 years after the event it portrayed – *The Rolling Stones Rock and Roll Circus* was finally released on CD, DVD and VHS. Recorded on December 11, 1968, the concert footage featured (besides the Stones themselves) The Who, Taj Mahal, Jethro Tull, Marianne Faithfull and ad hoc supergroup The Dirty Mac, comprising Keith, Mitch Mitchell, Eric Clapton, John Lennon and Yoko Ono. Intended for broadcast by the BBC, it was withheld at the time by the Stones who were unhappy with their performance.

During December of 1996 and January 1997, Mick and Keith worked up demos at Dangerous Music in New York before relocating to London in February to continue the process. By the time the extended band got together at Ocean Way Recording in Hollywood in March, producers The Dust Brothers and Danny Saber were on board and the sessions got going in earnest. Recording was finally completed at the end of July. The album was mastered on August 11 and a week later the four principals gathered in New York to announce the details of the forthcoming *Bridges To Babylon* tour, which would spread over two years and would not conclude until June 1999.

SEPTEMBER 27, 1997

Bridges To Babylon (Virgin V8447121 – LP; 8449092 - CD)

Flip The Switch/Anybody Seen My Baby?/Low Down/Already Over Me/Gunface/You Don't Have To Mean It/Out Of Control/Saint Of Me/Might As Well Get Juiced/Always Suffering/Too Tight/Thief In The Night/How Can I Stop

Disparate ways of working do not necessarily make a cohesive whole and that is certainly the case with *Bridges To Babylon*. With Mick having utilized the services of the aforementioned Dust Brothers and Danny Saber, his songs tended to have a more processed ambience while Keith's, who worked mainly with Don Was, had a more organic feel.

First single 'Anybody Seen My Baby?', a slightly menacing but otherwise unremarkable mid-tempo ballad, nearly got the band into hot water when Keith's daughter Angela noticed its similarity to k.d.lang's hit 'Constant Craving'. A legal battle was averted when Lang and her co-writer Ben Mink were given equal composer credits with Jagger and Richards. The promo video was notable for featuring a young Angelina Jolie.

Aside from a couple of inspired moments, including second single, 'Saint Of Me', the poppy reggae of 'You Don't Have To Mean It' (one of three Keith vocals on the album) and the lush ballad 'Already Over Me', it has to be said that *Bridges To Babylon* is a fairly mundane affair. 'Flip The Switch' and 'Gunface' are fairly perfunctory Stones rockers and are instantly forgettable, while 'Might As Well Get Juiced' is a good idea muddied by The Dust Brothers' production techniques.

Mick's desperation to be seen on the radar of the burgeoning dance market meant 'Out Of Control' and 'Saint Of Me' received a plethora of different mixes; Armand van Helden, Todd Terry and Deep Dish all got in on the act. One suspects Keith Richards gave the whole sorry episode an extremely wide berth.

Tour-tastic

1998 saw the gigantic *Bridges To Babylon* tour continue to criss-cross the globe. One of the features of the stage set-up was 'the bridge' which connected to a second, smaller stage sited around 150 metres into the middle of the arena. The set was designed by Mick and Charlie in conjunction with British architect Mark Fisher, who had previously worked with the likes of Pink Floyd (*The Wall*) and U2 (*Zoo TV*) as well as theatrical shows including Cirque du Soleil in Las Vegas and the Queen-inspired musical *We Will Rock You*. The second stage enabled the band to get closer to the bulk of the audience where they would perform three or four songs before retreating to the main stage.

Above: Don Was – producer of *Bridges To Babylon*.

Left: Signed set list from the Malaga show, July 16, 1998.

On November 1998 another Stones live album hit stores around the world. Entitled *No Security*, it had been recorded at a number of venues on the *Bridges To Babylon* tour. To differentiate it from more recent live albums, the band decided to include songs that had rarely been performed live, including 'Memory Motel', 'Waiting On A Friend' and 'Respectable'. There was also a cover of the Taj Mahal hit 'Corrina'. *No Security* holds the dubious distinction of being the worst-performing Rolling Stones album, chart-wise, in their whole catalogue. It barely registered in the UK chart, scraping into the top 75 for one week at 67.

The *Bridges To Babylon* tour finally wrapped on June 20, 1999, at the Mungersdorfer Stadium in Cologne, Germany. It had taken in 108 shows in the previous two years, including for the first time shows in Osaka, Moscow, Tallinn and Zagreb. All in all, it's estimated that the Stones had performed to more than four and a half million fans.

Above: Launching yet another mega tour, under the Brooklyn Bridge, New York, August 1997.

Right: Ronnie keeps on rocking ...

MICK JAGGER

Michael Philip Jagger was born on July 26, 1943, at the Livingstone Hospital in Dartford, Kent. His father Basil Fanshawe 'Joe' Jagger was a teacher (as was Mick's paternal grandfather), and his mother Eva Ensley Mary a hairdresser. Mick's younger brother Chris was born in December 1947.

Although Mick and Keith Richards attended primary school together they came from widely different backgrounds, Mick's being solidly middle-class, Keith's more working-class. Joe encouraged his son to pursue his interest in sport and physical education and Mick was an athletic teenager, excelling at basketball and cricket.

Like Keith, Mick took an interest in music from an early age. He loved to sing and would mimic the great rock'n'rollers of the time – Buddy Holly, Eddie Cochran, Elvis and Chuck Berry. Joe recalled, "I've never known a youngster with such an analytical approach to things. If he copied a song, he was able to capture the sound exactly."

The first album he remembers buying says a lot about the young Mick; it was *Muddy Waters At Newport*. By this time he was something of a purist and was also listening to the likes of Big Bill Broonzy, Sister Rosetta Tharpe and Leadbelly. He was so passionate about his music that he would save his pocket-money and order direct from Chess Records in Chicago.

In July 1961 Mick, having passed three 'A' levels, secured a place at the prestigious London School of Economics (LSE). On receiving his scholarship he signed a declaration that committed him to completing his course in economics and political science. This would all change, however, when he bumped into Keith on that fateful day a few months later.

As frontman of 'the greatest rock'n'roll band in the world', Mick's personal life has always come under scrutiny from a fascinated media worldwide. His dalliances with a series of famous and beautiful women helped sell newspapers worldwide, and right from his first publicised love affair in 1964 with model Chrissie Shrimpton (the younger sister of famous Sixties icon Jean Shrimpton), his romances have made front-page headlines.

In 1966, he famously took up with an already married Marianne Faithfull. Faithfull had been discovered by Stones manager Andrew Loog Oldham singing in a coffee bar a couple of years before and had launched her musical career with the Jagger/Richards song 'As Tears Go By'. Her continuing drug problems contributed

Above: Mick through the ages. Fresh faced in December 1963; photographed by Andy Warhol in 1975; getting his hair styled before a TV performance at the BBC in 1974; receiving his knighthood in December 2003.

Opposite: In the studio recording 'Sympathy For The Devil', 1968.

to their somewhat tempestuous relationship ending in May 1970.

In May 1971, Mick married Nicaraguan-born model and socialite Bianca Perez-Mora Macias. The pair had met at a party after a Stones show at the Palais des Sports in Paris. Their daughter Jade was born on October 21 of that year.

Mick's relationship with Bianca drove a wedge between him and Keith, who saw Bianca's influence over his bandmate as unhealthy and disruptive to the group's work ethic.

Their marriage was to be relatively short-lived, and with Bianca citing adultery (Mick had been seeing Texan model Jerry Hall for more than a year) they divorced in May 1978. Jerry Hall had made a name for herself as one of the first fashion supermodels, and after dating Roxy Music frontman Bryan Ferry had appeared on the cover of their album *Siren* in 1975. She had met Mick after a Stones show at Earls Court in May 1976 but the pair only started dating after meeting again at a mutual friend's dinner party in Manhattan the following year. They 'married' (the mainly Hindu ceremony was later deemed to be unlawful) on November 21, 1990, in Bali and officially separated (with Mick's infidelities again being cited as the reason) in 1999. The pair have four children together: Elizabeth, James, Georgia May and Gabriel. Mick also has children from two other brief liaisons: Karis (with American singer Marsha Hunt) and Lucas (with Brazilian fashion model Luciana Morad). Mick's girfriend, since 2001, was American stylist L'Wren Scott. She died tragically – ruled as a suicide by New York authorities – in March 2014.

Outside of The Rolling Stones, Mick's solo career has been fair to middling. His last album, *Goddess In The Doorway* (caustically re-christened *Dogshit In The Doorway* by a certain K Richards Esq.) was released in 2001 and almost universally panned by the critics. However, it racked up enough sales (60,000 units) to warrant silver status in the UK. The making of the album was accompanied by the rather self-aggrandizing documentary *Being Mick*, which aired on network television in the UK and US.

Mick has also pursued an on-off acting career. His most credible and critically acclaimed role came in 1970 with the release of *Performance*, British directors Donald Cammell and Nicholas Roeg's cult masterpiece, filmed in 1968, in which he starred alongside Anita Pallenberg and James Fox. Following this he played the eponymous lead in Tony Richardson's *Ned Kelly*, released in 1970. However, the filming was dogged by problems and disowned by both Richardson and Jagger. Since then there have been minor roles in projects as diverse as the Sci-Fi epic *Freejack* (1992), *Bent* (1997 – as a Berlin transvestite) and *The Man From Elysian Fields* (2002).

December 12, 2003, saw Michael Philip Jagger, one-time scourge of the British establishment, attend a ceremony at Buckingham Palace to be awarded his knighthood. Keith, of course, was disparaging in the extreme, claiming 'It's not what the Stones is about, is it?'.

Left: Stevie Wonder joins Mick Jagger onstage in 1972, to duet 'Satisfaction', and to celebrate Mick's 29th birthday.

Right: "The most famous rock and roll singer in the world", accompanied by his band – and Ian Stewart on piano – at an early show in 1962.

2000 AND ONWARDS:
LICKS AND A BIGGER BANG

In May 2002 the Stones assembled in Paris to record some new material that would augment their greatest hits on the forthcoming double album. *Forty Licks* would be their first career-spanning 'best of' and would mark the band's 40th anniversary –a rock 'n' roll first. A joint venture between Virgin and ABKCO, the double CD would be split equally between the Klein back catalogue and their post-1971 output. It would prove to be a masterstroke, as *Forty Licks* would go on to sell more than six million copies worldwide.

The *Licks* tour which accompanied the release of the album would also see a new approach to touring, with the band playing three distinct sizes of venue in most of the major cities they visited: stadium, indoor arena and club. This was never more clearly illustrated than at the start of the European leg of the tour in Munich, where they played the gigantic Olympiastadion, the indoor Olympiahalle and the tiny Circus Krone. In an attempt to keep themselves as fresh as possible the Stones rehearsed more than 50 songs, with the result that the set often changed radically from show to show. This meant they could also feature a key album every night and these included *Let It Bleed*, *Sticky Fingers* and *Exile On Main Street*.

By the time the Licks tour wound up in Hong Kong in September 2003, a full 12 months after it had begun, the band had played 117 shows across five continents.

The *Licks* tour was chronicled on the sumptuous *Four Flicks* four-DVD box set, released in November 2003. The set featured three complete shows: an arena show (Madison Square Garden, New York), a stadium show (Twickenham stadium, London) and a theatre show (L'Olympia, Paris). There was also a documentary and extras which featured band and crew interviews. Another double live album was also released, the rather superfluous *Live Licks*.

In March 2003, after only four months off, the Stones again chose Paris to meet up to discuss future plans. However, this time there were to be two rather large flies in the ointment. Shortly after the meeting Charlie was diagnosed with throat cancer. Thankfully he made a full recovery, but it meant that any further touring plans would have to put on hold. It was also revealed that Ronnie was having treatment for his alcohol addiction and that his doctor had warned him to give up smoking or risk major health problems within the next couple of years. With the other two indisposed, The Glimmer Twins decided to carry on regardless and, billeted at Mick's chateau in the Loire Valley, settled down to write new material together.

Top left: Signed (by the band and Martin Scorsese) promotional Fender Telecaster for the *Shine A Light* movie.

Left: Munich, June 5, 2003. The band at a press conference marking the start of the *Forty Licks* tour.

SEPTEMBER 5, 2005

A Bigger Bang (Virgin V3012)

Rough Justice/Let Me Down Slow/It Won't Take Long/Rain Fall Down/Streets Of Love/Back Of My Hand/She Saw Me Coming/Biggest Mistake/This Place Is Empty/Oh No, Not You Again/Dangerous Beauty/Laugh, I Nearly Died/Sweet Neo Con/Look What The Cat Dragged In/Driving Too Fast/Infamy

Charlie's illness had the effect of galvanizing Mick and Keith, and the songwriting sessions the previous summer proved enormously productive. So, with Charlie fully recovered (Ronnie was still absent at this point) the trio, with Don Was again in the producer's chair, began recording in earnest, again at Mick's house in Poce-sur-Cisse, France.

The album was finally completed at Ocean Way Recording in LA at the end of June, just two weeks before tour rehearsals were due to start in Toronto. On September 5, a mere eight years on from their last studio album, *A Bigger Bang* finally hit the stores.

In an effort to stop the album leaking on to the internet, initial review copies were sent out in a protected CDR format, housed in a plain printed sleeve and credited to 'The Little Wonders' – a nod to Ian Stewart's nickname for the band. As usual, critics were quick to a label it as a major return to form; many went as far as to say that it was their best album since 1978's *Some Girls*. In truth, it's half a great album and, at 16 songs and 64 minutes, far too long. 'Back Of My Hand' is an authentic return to the band's blues roots and although it sounds somewhat out of place, is a lot of fans' favourite track. 'Biggest Mistake' sounds like it's been teleported from *Aftermath* and is the nearest the album gets to pop, while 'Streets Of Love' can stand proudly next to the likes of 'Fool To Cry' and 'Memory Motel'. The tour which accompanied the album was another mammoth trek around the world's sports stadia. It took in mainland China for the first time, with a show in Shanghai, where the band performed to a slightly bemused mix of high-ranking Communist party officials and wealthy Western businessmen. Two smaller shows at the Beacon Theatre in New York were filmed by Martin Scorsese to form the basis for the *Shine A Light* documentary film that opened in April 2008.

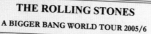
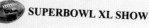

THE ROLLING STONES
A BIGGER BANG WORLD TOUR 2005/6

SUN, FEB 5, 2006   SHOW # 54   DETROIT FORD FIELD

SUPERBOWL XL SHOW

1	START ME UP		BV+BC GTR	Off stage	F	120
2	ROUGH JUSTICE		BF	Off Stage	D	138
3	SATISFACTION		BV+BC GTR	Off stage	E	134

Below: Live at the Beacon Theatre, New York, November 1, 2006, filming the *Shine A Light* movie.

Above: Superbowl XL set list, February 2006.

Right: Ronnie, Mick and Keith performing in Hanover's Open Air Arena, August 8, 2003 on the *Forty Licks* tour.

Overleaf: Fully signed poster from the press conference to announce the *Bridges To Babylon* tour NYC, 1997.

PICTURE CREDITS

The publishers would like to thank the following sources for their kind permission to reproduce the pictures in this book.

Key: t = top, b = bottom, l = left, r = right and c = centre

Alamy Images: /Interfoto: 28l, 28r, /Pictorial Press Ltd.: 9t

© Carlton Books: /Karl Adamson: 10l, 10br, 11l, 11r, 12tl, 12r, 12b, 13, 21tr, 30, 31tl, 31tr, 31bl, 43br, 48tl, 48tr, 48bl, 49tl, 49br, 50, 51, 54-55, 59r, 81tr, 91tc, 92-93, 94tr

Corbis: 8br, 14r, 15tr, 16bc, 18bl, 19bc, 21l, 23br, 29tr, 38bc, 40tr, 41r, 52t, 53r, 58tr, 59br, 63c, 79tc, 80bl, 84br, 90t; /Bettmann: 39, 46b, 58l, 65; /Henry Diltz: 33b; /Pierre Fournier/Sygma: 19tl; /Lynn Goldsmith: 53tr, 53l, 86l; / Hulton-Deutsch Collection: 19tr, 34-35; /Neal Preston: 41l, 62l; / Image © The Andy Warhol Foundation: 86r (2)

Dagmar/www.dagmarfoto.com: 37tl, 44b

Getty Images: 8l, 15bl, 16c, 21br, 22, 23t, 23bl, 23r, 27t, 29bl, 32, 37b, 40tc, 47bl, 47br, 59tr, 60-61, 63br, 66br, 76b, 79r, 86r (1), 87, 90b; /AFP: 74, 80tc, 85t, 86r (4); / Waring Abbot: 44b; /DDP: 91r; /Lichfield: 45b; /Michael Ochs Archive: 17tc, 17b, 19br, 20b, 20tr, 29tc, 33t, 38l,

44t, 88; /Terry 'O'Neill: 4; /Popperfoto: 14l, 38br, 72; / Redferns: 2, 6b, 7r, 9b, 17tr, 19tc, 20tl, 21c, 38t, 40b, 42-43, 47tl, 63tl, 67r, 69br, 81b, 89; /Time & Life Pictures: 21tl; /Wireimage: 57, 62r, 68, 69bl, 70-71, 75t, 78, 80-81, 82, 83

Mirrorpix.com: 17l, 24-25, 26, 27br, 37tc, 37tr, 76l, 94b, 95

Photoshot: /Michael Putland/Retna UK: 46t, 52c, 53br, 67l, 73l; /Gary Reshoff/Retna UK: 59l; /Retna UK: 45t, 64, 66bc, 73r, 75c, 77

Rex Features: 18r; /Everett Collection/Buena Vista: 78bl; / Everett Collection/Paramount: 91bl; /Dezo Hoffmann: 6t, 7l, 8r, 56l; /O'Neill: 27l; /Terry O'Neill: 86r (3); /Brian Rasic: 85br; /John Schute/Daily Mail: 56r; /Sipa Press: 36; / Startracks Photo: 84r; /Richard Young: 75bl

Memorabilia courtesy of Matt Lee

Every effort has been made to acknowledge correctly and contact the source and/or copyright holder of each picture and Carlton Books Limited apologises for any unintentional errors or omissions, which will be corrected in future editions of this book.

Right: Backstage pass.

Below: Mick on Ronnie on the up, European tour 1982.

Opposite: The infamous appearance on *Juke Box Jury*, June 1964.

Overleaf: The band in 1965, as many of their fans will fondly remember them at their very best.

Rolling ★★★
★★★ Stones
ACCESS
Backstage &
Dressing Rooms

NAME   Authorised Signature